PENG

DEVLOK WITH DEVDUTT PATTANAIK 2

Devdutt Pattanaik writes, illustrates and lectures on the relevance of mythology in modern times. He has, since 1996, written over 30 books and 700 columns on how stories, symbols and rituals construct the subjective truth (myths) of ancient and modern cultures around the world.

BY THE SAME AUTHOR

Myth=Mithya: Decoding Hindu Mythology

The Book of Ram

The Pregnant King

Jaya: An Illustrated Retelling of the Mahabharata

Sita: An Illustrated Retelling of the Ramayana

Shikhandi and Other Queer Tales They Don't Tell You

Jaya Colouring Book

Sita Colouring Book

Devlok with Devdutt Pattanaik

Olympus: An Indian Retelling of the Greek Myths

DEVLOK

with Devdutt Pattanaik

2

PENGUIN BOOKS

PENGUIN BOOKS

USA | Canada | UK | Ireland | Australia
New Zealand | India | South Africa | China

Penguin Books is part of the Penguin Random House group of companies
whose addresses can be found at global.penguinrandomhouse.com

Published by Penguin Books India Pvt. Ltd
7th Floor, Infinity Tower C, DLF Cyber City,
Gurgaon 122 002, Haryana, India

First published by Penguin Books India 2017

10 9 8 7 6 5 4 3 2 1

The views and opinions expressed in this book are the author's own and the facts are as reported by him which have been verified to the extent possible, and the publishers are not in any way liable for the same.

ISBN 9780143428435

Typeset in AJensonPro by Manipal Digital Systems, Manipal
Printed at Replika Press Pvt. Ltd, India

www.penguin.co.in

Contents

Author's Note

- This is a collection of easy-going conversations about Indian mythology, based on the eponymous television show
- What is discussed here is not meant to be factually 'accurate'—you may refer to your guru for clarity
- This is not an academic work and does not claim to be authoritative
- Contained here are simplified versions of mythological tales, taken from various versions found in different scriptures and in folklore
- The attempt is to retain the essence embedded in the tales, and to provoke readers to dig deeper into the philosophy
- I offer here a subjective truth, *my* truth, which is one among many truths, because:

> Within infinite myths lies an eternal truth
>
> Who knows it all?
>
> Varuna has but a thousand eyes
>
> Indra, a hundred
>
> You and I, only two

1

Dhyan and Darshan

In this new season, what should we start with?

We'll talk about the Vedas and the Puranas, of course, stories from the Ramayana and the Mahabharata, but before that, let's talk about the poem that I begin all my projects with.

When I started writing books twenty years ago, all my books would open with the lines:

> Within infinite myths lies the eternal truth.
> Who sees it all?
> Varuna has but a thousand eyes,
> Indra has a hundred,
> And I, only two . . .

I used to say 'the' eternal truth, where 'the' is the definitive article. Now I say 'an' eternal truth. The concept that Varuna has a thousand eyes is found in the Vedas, and the idea that Indra has a hundred eyes comes from the Puranas. Earlier, I would say 'And I'; gradually, I began to write 'You and I'.

As my knowledge increased, my point of view, or darshan, which is different for different people, changed. And as we meditate (dhyan) on things, our knowledge increases. In twenty years, as my darshan and dhyan changed significantly, so did the poem.

This is a good point to start the new season with: dhyan and darshan. What is darshan?

Ordinarily, people would say darshan is 'to see'. When we go to a temple, we take darshan of god. In films, you will hear dialogues like, 'Bhagwan, darshan do [Lord, let me see you].' So, darshan is given and taken—both to do with seeing. In Sanskrit, darshan means philosophy or world view.

Dhyan means to pay attention, concentrate, focus.

There is a reason why I use the words dhyan and darshan separately. In India's history, the Vedas came 4000 years ago, and the Puranas, 2000 years ago. The Vedas contain poetry associated with yagna while in the Puranas stories became very important. The idea of dhyan lies somewhere in between these two. In yagna parampara, or tradition, people followed the rituals, did karmakaand, but they began to ask what these meant. That is, people started thinking about it; they started concentrating—this is known as dhyan.

But it was Buddha who made dhyan really important. He belonged to the Shraman parampara, people who were vairagis (ascetics), philosophers—they were not worldly, and lived in the forest, caves, or viharas (monasteries). Buddha said that performing the rituals and penance (tap)—in the form of fasting, physical hardship—alone would not bring knowledge. They would have to mull over, meditate about it. He gave a lot of importance to dhyan—sit in one place, close your eyes, stay still and do dhyan.

Dhyan has several meanings. One is to contemplate or to think. Another is to not think but to meditate, wherein you stay still and automatically you'll get kaivalya gyan, or wisdom. The more you think, the farther you'll go from wisdom. There are two schools of dhyan—mindful (contemplation) and mindless (meditation).

Closing the eyes is associated with dhyan. Its opposite is darshan—opening the eyes.

Post the Shraman tradition, in the Puranic period, when we start telling stories, when temples are established, the word darshan becomes popular. The Vedas give greater importance to shruti, to hear, while the Puranas emphasize seeing. If you observe the idols in temples, they have large eyes—Lord Jagannath has big, round eyes, Shrinathji has boat-like eyes. In poetry too—Varuna has a thousand eyes, Indra one hundred, and so on. We see god, god sees us. God is presenting himself to us.

Another theory is that dhyan was perhaps associated with sanyasis who were removed from the world and its relationships, whereas darshan was about relationships. About seeing the person opposite you—your brother, sister, wife. With the Ramayana and the Mahabharata, family stories emerge, of the parents, brothers, wives of the protagonists. Society and relationships are important here.

Dhyan and darshan are two opposite concepts. One is external, the other, internal.

Dhyan is about vairagi life, and is Buddhist, while darshan is about worldly life, and is Hindu. This is the basis of Sanatan Dharma.

You keep using the word 'mythology', which upsets some people. Why do you use this word?

This is not a new word, it's hundreds of years old. But the British gave it a negative meaning. I say it's a colonial meaning where myth is equated with lies. In the twenty-first century, its meaning is different. We should abandon the colonial meaning and adopt the contemporary meaning—neeji satya, vyaktigat satya, mera sach, tumhara sach, meaning one's personal truth. *That* is myth. When I say mythology, I want people to absorb the new meaning of the word. In English, fact means everyone's truth; fiction is imaginary stories (sabka jhoot). Where would you place the Ramayana and the Mahabharata? A scientist would not be sure about its reality, and say there's no evidence. But if you say it's fiction, a believer is likely to get annoyed, 'How can you call our god fiction?' In between fact and fiction lies vishwas (faith), which is somebody's truth. When you form a relationship with someone, you have to respect their truth. In earlier times, when there was sanatan satya, they never said something is right or wrong. The Brahmand is eternal, while we have limited lifespans, barely 100 years. The world is anadi, anant, without beginning or end, and we can never know everything.

We all have different kinds of knowledge, but we must keep gathering more and expand our mind (mann). Take darshan of all these truths and think (dhyan) about it so that your mind expands. Mann is manas and in Sanskrit, to expand is brah. So Brahman is to expand your mind. That's the original meaning of the word.

Myth is a Greek word. It means story. Istor, the Greek word for history, means story as well. Thus, in Greek, myth and history have the same meaning. If I say I saw a peacock dancing in the forest, and you ask me for proof, I may have none. But I will have the experience, the anubhav of it. You might think it's false, but it's real to me. So is my truth true or not? Likewise, if I say I've experienced god, and I'm asked to prove it, I won't be able to. Does my experience become false then?

Rama is an anubhav; Shri Krishna is an anubhav. I am not even interested in proof. I've experienced it and am telling you a story based on it. What you see (darshan) and pay attention to (dhyan) tells of your sophistication too. Are you violent (hinsak), refusing to believe me, or do you believe in non-violence (ahinsak), and are able to absorb my truth? In Jainism, there are Anekant-vaad (different truths) and Syaad-vaad (partial truth or ardhsatya, half-truth). This brings humility in a person. This is sanatan parampara which we are now losing.

We've been blessed with many lives to continue gaining knowledge. Anant in mathematics is infinity. There is no measure for it, but by using it so many problems are solved. Similarly, truth that is based on faith helps us solve life's problems, not scientific truth.

Would you say darshan is more important or dhyan?

Both are important. Darshan makes me see the truths of others. Dhyan helps me 'cook' all these in my mind. One is input, the other is processing. There are people who hold on to one idea and are not willing to listen to any other facts or truths. They do not do darshan or dhyan; instead they become violent, saying, 'You are wrong, what *I* say is the truth,' and so on.

Dhyan by itself will not allow you to see other truths, because everything is not on the inside alone; some of it is outside as well. In temples, there are idols of couples (dampattya) like Shiva and Gauri looking at each other—darshan. The meaning is layered. Is one looking at the other's body, property, heart, mind or soul? There's darshan on which I've meditated (dhyan) and so I have good relationships.

Are there any stories related to dhyan and darshan?

There are a few which are associated with temples. Puri temple has a story in which a devotee wants darshan of the god but the pujari does not allow him in, so the god comes to the door. There's an idol at the door of Puri temple called Patitapavan where god gives darshan to those devotees who are not permitted inside the temple.

In Tirupati, there's a story about a yogi called Hathiram, who goes into the temple so often that the priests become suspicious and stop him from entering. So he sits outside and it is said that each night, god comes to play chausar with him. You'll find many of these idols in Tirupati.

There's a similar story in Udupi in Karnataka. Kanakdas is a devotee of Krishna and wants to take his darshan at a particular temple. However, he is turned away at the door by upper-caste priests on the suspicion that he belongs to a lower caste. So he pitches a tent in front of the temple and sits there chanting and writing a bhajan in Krishna's name. A priest comes and violently removes him from there. The next morning, Kanakdas finds that an earthquake the night before has destroyed the wall of the temple, leaving the idol exposed, and thus open for worship.

All these stories indicate how god gives his darshan to his devotees, whether by coming out of the temple or turning around. After getting darshan, one should do dhyan on it.

Do you give darshan to people? How do you treat and interact with people? You should think about what kind of darshan you give others. Do we also build walls around us and do not reveal ourselves? Do we show only one aspect of our personality? This knowledge will only come through dhyan. You gather data through darshan. To tie it all in and find meaning you need dhyan.

Can it be said that the rishis who did tapasya were doing dhyan?

Rishis close their eyes and meditate, but they have isolated themselves from society. In stories, when those who have closed their eyes for many days finally open them, flames burst forth from their eyes. Kapila Muni burns the sons of Sagar that way. When Gandhari opens her eyes after many years of being blindfolded, her glance sets Yudhishtira's feet on fire. If you do not look at the person before you (darshan), and are only in dhyan, the relationship breaks. It's a horrific roop.

There's a famous story of Shiva in which he opens his third eye and emits fire. Parvati comes and slowly opens his two other eyes so that he can do darshan and balance dhyan and darshan. When he opens only one eye, he is Kamantaka, the one who destroys Kama, the god of love, but when he opens both eyes and sees Parvati, he calms down and marries her (Kamakshi). So dhyan is internal, darshan is external, and we go from one to the other. It's a cyclical movement.

2

Amrita Manthan

Recently, at Bangkok airport I saw this huge, interesting installation depicting Amrita manthan. Where did this story originate?

This story first originated in the Mahabharata; it's also in the Ramayana, the Vishnu Purana, the Shiva Purana, in loka kathas, or folk tales. It's a very popular story. The structure of the Angkor Wat Temple in Cambodia depicts the story of the Amrita manthan.

So this story appears in the mythologies of other countries as well?

Yes. There were trade relations between India and South Asian countries. Ships carried masalas, cloth, etc., and along with this our stories also spread. You'll find Puranic stories in South East Asia too.

What's the meaning of the word Amrita?

A-mrita, that is, something by which there will be no death (mrityu). Basically Amrita gives immortality. All human beings desire a world where there's no death. It is said that earlier the devas also used to die and were scared of death; so, they were looking for Amrita.

There are many versions of this story, which is quite long. The one I know begins with Indra. Can you tell us the story?

Indra lives in heaven which has everything—the Kalpataru (wish-fulfilling tree), Kamadhenu (wish-fulfilling cow), Chintamani (wish-fulfilling jewel). He is such a hedonistic king that one day when Rishi Durvasa comes to him, Indra doesn't pay attention to the sage. The rishi is carrying a beautiful necklace as a gift for the deva. Indra takes it and throws it to the floor and his elephant, Airavata, walks over it. Upset at Indra's insolence, the rishi curses that Indra will lose all his wealth. Lakshmi, the goddess of wealth and prosperity who sits in heaven, is dissolved in the Kshir Sagar. Indra has nothing left.

In distress, he goes to his father, Brahma, who takes him to Vishnu. Vishnu tells him everything has dissolved in the Kshir Sagar, so he'll have to work to get it back. First, he would have to make a churn (manthan); then, befriend the asuras (demons, enemies of the devas). This is how enterprise begins. The picture shows asuras on one side, devas on the other, churning the ocean. It's not a tug-of-war as some people think. When both sides pull at the same time, that's a sign of conflict. That's devasura sangram, war between devas and asuras. If you and I speak at the same time, the one whose voice is louder will prevail. That's tug-of-war. But in a manthan, when one party pulls, the other waits. The philosophical concept of cooperation is at work here. Amrita manthan is the first time that devas and asuras cooperate, which leads to samvaad, conversation. This no longer exists today. Because there's only tug-of-war, and no manthan, you don't see Amrita in today's society!

What is the Kshir Sagar?

Kshir means doodh or milk in Sanskrit. The word kheer comes from kshir. The Kshir Sagar refers to an ocean of milk. It's a concept, a flight of fancy—can there really be an ocean of milk? Milk is important in our economy. Cows are worshipped and milk is considered one of the most important sources of nutrition; it gives butter, curds, ghee. It's a powerful concept because there is no limit/boundary to the Kshir Sagar. In an ordinary ocean, you must stop at a port. But this is a fetterless, limitless, anant sagar. One might say it's a metaphor for Bhudevi, the earth. When you churn it, you get grain, metal, which you have to work for to obtain—through agriculture, mining, and so on.

Another way we can look at this is that the mind is the Kshir Sagar. If you meditate, do tapasya, many good things can emerge from the mind.

But manthan is important. Two opposing forces have to work in cooperation, not in conflict. For example, left brain and right brain. When one brain works, the other is quiet. This balance, which we often forget, is very important.

The churning rod in this story is the Mandar Parvat, and the rope is the naga king Vasuki?

Some say Meru Parvat, but whatever the name, parvat (mountain) is important. The churning rope is sometimes Vasuki, sometimes Adi Shesh. Here, the mountain implies space (sthal) and the serpent symbolizes time (kaal). So time and space are being used to churn the ocean of milk. Philosophically, allegorically, it's a complex story. Both space and time are being used, as is matter, or kshir.

Garuda, the king of eagles, brings the mountain, and Vasuki acts as the rope. But without a base, the mountain will sink, so Vishnu takes the Kurma avatar, the turtle, to form the base. The Vedas call the Kurma avatar Akupar. Why turtle? First, because it floats. Second, it's a symbol of yoga. It can withdraw its head and legs into its shell, like a rishi can control his senses (indriyan) during tapasya. So if you have to do manthan, the knowledge of yoga—the ability to control the senses—is important.

Indra, who does not practise control, loses Lakshmi. Keeping the indriyan in control can restore Lakshmi—an avataran of her is possible. Just like a fruit has a kernel which is very potent, this story too has a lot of philosophy packed inside it.

Indra invites the asuras to the churning. Why is that?

Today one political party would ideally not want any other party around—no opposition. But that's not how the world works. You have to work with everyone. You have to befriend your enemies too. Likewise, in the Amrita manthan, the collaboration of devas and asuras is an important element. Devas are said to be afraid of the serpent so they stay on the side of its tail and the asuras near its head. In stories, the devas are usually depicted as weaker and more cautious, whereas asuras are strong and confident. So this force and counter force continues for many yugas. Slowly, like you get butter from milk, different treasures (ratna) emerge from the Kshir Sagar.

What emerged from the Kshir Sagar after the manthan?

The list changes from one Purana to another. Traditionally it's believed that fourteen ratna emerged. In a wedding ceremony, when they chant the mantra describing marriage as a manthan, it is wished that these fourteen jewels also emerge from the couple's marriage. These are symbols of dharma (governance, law), artha (economics) and kama (pleasure, bhog).

During the manthan, the symbols of dharma that emerge are the elephant Airavata, the horse Ucchaishrava and the bow Saranga. These are symbols of a king, who is responsible for dharma—to determine people's role and responsibilities in society, to maintain law and order, etc. The symbols of artha that emerge are the cow Kamadhenu, the Kalpataru or Parijat tree and the Chintamani or Kaustubh jewel—animal wealth, plant wealth and mineral wealth. The symbols of kama or pleasure that emerge are the handsome and romantic Chandra, the beautiful and talented apsaras and the musicians or gandharvas. Though some are unsure since it is a controversial item, wine or alcohol (varuni or soma rasa), and Nidradevi (sleep), because sleep gives pleasure, are also believed to have emerged from the Kshir Sagar.

All these are then divided among the devas and asuras: one wants the horse, another the elephant, and so on. The concept of division (batwara) begins from here. As in a business, while there is collaboration in the effort, when it is time to share the profits, disputes break out about who will get what percentage—so it happens between devas and asuras.

Importantly, Lakshmi too emerged from the Kshir Sagar. She combines dharma, artha and kama. She sits on a lotus, is surrounded by apsaras and gandharvas, and she wears a lotus necklace (vyjayantimala). It is said that anyone who wears this necklace will always be victorious. After the manthan, the devas and the asuras both wish to marry her, but she says she will choose her own husband. She chooses Vishnu who had come up with the idea of collaboration, and managed to make two opposing forces work with each other.

Interestingly, when an enterprise brings treasures, it also brings problems. There is a dark element to this story as well. Several versions exist. One says that the trees on the mountain rub against each other and their friction causes fire, which produces smoke. The snake inhales that smoke and starts vomiting. When all this smoke, fire, vomit, and the tears in the eyes of the devas mix with the Kshir Sagar, poison or halahal is created. Neither the devas nor the asuras want this. Vishnu wonders what is to be done now. There's only one being who can swallow it all and that's the deva of devas, Mahadeva, or Shiva. He is Bholenath, the innocent one, and he does not care whether it's milk or poison. He starts to drink it. He is a vairagi, an ascetic, but his wife, Parvati, is worldly (samsarik). She protests: How can you give my husband poison? She squeezes Shiva's throat to stop him from swallowing the poison, so it just sits there. He becomes Neelkantha, the blue-throated one. Philosophically, the idea is that work will bring with it problems, which, like Shiva, you should have the ability to absorb, else you will not progress.

There's always a concept of balance at play: force–counter force, nectar–poison, ascetic–worldly, etc.

Now, everything else has emerged, and the climax of the story is the appearance of Amrita. The commonest version of this story is that a god known as Dhanvantari emerges, bearing a pot of Amrita. Both devas and asuras rush towards it and start fighting for it. Eventually, Vishnu assumes the form of a beautiful apsara, Mohini, and deceitfully takes away the pot and gives all the Amrita to the devas.

I've heard that the Kumbh Mela is associated with the Amrita manthan story.

It is believed that at the Kumbh Mela, after the shahi snan (noble bath), the river becomes like Amrita, and if you bathe in this water, you'll absorb the qualities of Amrita. All your paap (sin) and bad karma will be washed away and you'll start with a clean slate. It is also believed that when the pot of Amrita was being carried towards heaven, a few drops fell to the earth—at Haridwar, Prayag in Allahabad, Nasik and Ujjain. That's why the Kumbh Melas are held here.

When both devas and asuras worked on the manthan, why were the asuras cheated out of the Amrita?

The argument about this goes on forever. One simple, rather dissatisfactory, answer is that the devas are good, the asuras bad, so the good should benefit. But this doesn't carry any philosophical depth. Another is about who started the enterprise. It began with the devas. The one who starts the enterprise brings everyone else in, so the fruit should go to the yajman, who'll then decide how it is to be divided. Here, Indra is the yajman.

There is another aspect to this. When devas and asuras are fighting, Vishnu becomes Mohini and tricks them with beauty. The asuras aren't aware that Mohini is pouring Amrita only in the mouths of the devas. Only one asura, Rahu, notices this. He stands among the devas and receives some Amrita. When Vishnu realizes this, he beheads the asura with his

Sudarshan chakra—the head becomes Rahu and the body becomes Ketu. On the face of it, this is unfair. But while Vishnu gives the devas Amrita and immortality, he does not give them paramsukh, supreme happiness. Worldly pleasures and wealth cannot bring happiness. So who has actually been cheated? The devas merely got immortality, the enjoyment of bhog, not happiness. A philosophical gap has emerged here. In a move that complicates things further, Shiva grants the asuras Sanjivani Vidya, the knowledge by which they can bring a dead person back to life. So the devas have Amrita, the asuras have Sanjivani Vidya. Whether this will result in a manthan or a tug-of-war is an eternal question.

3

Forest and Field

There is repeated mention of van, forest, in the epics—in the Ramayana, Rama goes to a forest for exile, while Krishna is associated with Vrindavan. Why is the van so important in our texts?

It's a basic part of Indian philosophy. Until we understand what this is, we cannot fully comprehend Indian sampradaya and parampara. Van refers to prakriti, or nature, where there is no human intervention, and everything is in its natural form. There are no rules. The stronger creatures survive—survival of the fittest, also called matsya nyaya in Sanskrit. The bigger fish eats the smaller one and that's not wrong or a sin.

Van is the most natural form of existence. Man comes and changes this pristine state of being. He establishes villages, farms and controls the land. He decides which tree will live and which will die. He decides which seeds to plant, what is crop and what is weed. He creates boundaries; he brings fire and marks a space for havan (fire worship), another for his village, and so on—basically, he assumes control of the ecosystem.

This division, with the van or aranya on one side, and the village, town, fields on the other, separates prakriti and sanskriti. Prakriti does not have rules; only nature's rules or laws. In man's world, you have concepts of neeti, niyam (morals, laws), riwaz (customs), nyaya and nyayadheesh (justice, judge), and property. This separation of two worlds is the fundamental principle of Indian philosophy.

When was this concept first introduced?

It was first mentioned in the Sama Veda 3500 years ago. The songs of the Sama Veda are of two kinds—Aranyageya Gaan (songs for prakriti) and Gramageya Gaan (songs for sanskriti). The grama will feature rules of family, kul, jati, varna and rajya (clan, caste, category and kingdom), that is, manushya or human rules. In prakriti there are no rules. This is mentioned again and again in the Sama Veda. In the Puranas, this has been elaborated further through stories and characters.

In the Ramayana and the Mahabharata, Rama and the Pandavas are sent to vanavas (life in the forest) as a form of punishment. Why?

In a sanskriti, there are yajman who perform yagna with Brahmins. Anyone who does not want to live in this sanskriti, goes into vanavas. After completing his householder duties, he goes into the forest, into vanaprastha ashram, and becomes a sanyasi/tapasvi/shraman/yogi. This is a voluntary movement. In Jainism, a Tirthankara who is born to royalty goes to the forest after completing his duties; he leaves everything behind, even his clothes, becomes a digambara (one who wears the sky) and goes into the forest. Buddha too goes to the forest to meditate on the cause of suffering.

But, in the Puranic stories of the Ramayana and the Mahabharata, going to the forest is a punishment. Staying in the city is a good thing; it has everything—rules, security, wealth, prosperity. When Rama is in Ayodhya, he is a prince; in the forest, he has no position, no status, no servants, belongings, no concept of dharma, rules, justice.

In the story where Lakshmana draws a line (Lakshmana-rekha) before leaving Sita to go and find Rama, the Lakshmana-rekha represents maryada, or boundary. Within it is the village, town, Rama's rules, where she is Rama's wife. The word patni (wife) is only applicable in sanskriti, not prakriti; there are no marriages or sanskar (morals) in a jungle. Once she crosses the boundary, she is no longer Rama's wife because there are no rules, no neeti or nyaya beyond the line. Ravana, who is a Veda gyani (knowledgeable about the Vedas), knows this difference. So Ravana will say, I committed no crime. Sita crossed the line of her own volition, which means she gave up her 'wife' status voluntarily. I just picked up a girl from the jungle, where matsya nyaya applies. He does this by deceit. This story can be connected with the Sama Veda and the separation between grama and van or aranya. This contrast often appears in stories.

What is the significance of the van in the Mahabharata?

In the Mahabharata this concept has a more sophisticated meaning. In the Ramayana, Rama is from the grama, he goes to the forest for his education, comes back and gets married and is sent back to the forest for his exile. After he returns to the palace, Sita is again sent to the forest—the story keeps switching between the village and the forest.

In the Mahabharata, however, the Pandavas go first from the forest, where they were born, to Hastinapur for education; there their house is burnt down and they go back to the forest. Then they marry Draupadi, turn Khandavprastha into Indraprastha, become kings, lose their kingdom in a game of dice and go back to the jungle. When they go to the city next, it's for war at Kurukshetra. They regain what they'd lost and, in the end, give that in daan (charity) and return to the forest—vanaprastha—where they die.

Each time they are in the forest, their attitude is different. The first time, they have nothing, they don't know that they're princes and are happy. The second time they're unhappy, because their palace has been burnt, and they have lost their kingdom; the third time too they're unhappy because they've lost everything in a game of dice. The fourth time, they have become more philosophical; they know fortune comes and goes and that in the jungle, nothing belongs to anybody. This is shown repeatedly during their exile.

Even a prince is just another creature in the forest. Shiva in the form of Keerat and Hanuman as a monkey repeatedly teach them this lesson that even if you burn down a forest and claim it as your kingdom—your land from where you get your power and ego—it is only maya, not the truth. You are creating an indrajaal, a delusion, and getting trapped in it.

Prakriti existed before your samaj (society) came into being and will continue even after it is gone.

What is the significance of the van in the Bhagavata Purana?

It tells the story of Krishna. He is born in Mathura, and is then taken across the river to cowherds in Gokul. Cowherds have no home, no basti where they settle; they wander with their cattle. That's who Krishna becomes.

Vrind means tulsi so Vrindavan is a fragrant tulsi van. The jungle is a dangerous place, since you could become someone's food any time. It's an insecure place as you can be attacked by snakes, scorpions, ants, mosquitoes, etc., who will not care that you're a prince. Krishna makes even such a dangerous place secure and happy. He doesn't destroy the forest and impose rules. He inhabits it and you feel it has become fragrant—Vrindavan, Madhuban (like honey).

Raas-leela always happens in a van at night, when women leave their husbands, children, fathers behind in the village, wear ornaments, and dance around Krishna. It suggests that when god is with you there'll be 'jungle mein mangal', joy even in a forest. When the most frightening place, where you have no rights or protection, becomes a happy liberating space for women, that's a sign of god's presence.

How is Shiva related to the van?

In the Buddhist tradition, Buddha left his palace and civilization (kshetra) and went to the forest and attained enlightenment. He established another world which is internal. The transition was from civilized society to the jungle and from the jungle to the mind. One of the meanings of the word nirvana is 'away from the jungle' (nir-vana).

Shiva's story is the opposite. He lives on icy, rocky mountaintops, far even from jungles, and is brought into civilization by Devi; he becomes Shankara and marries. He comes to Kashi, has a family, but every time there is a disagreement with his wife—the famous quarrel of Uma and Mahesh—he retreats into the deodar forest. This is the forest associated with him.

How is Shakti related to the van?

Prakriti is considered a form of Devi. When we refer to the jungle/aranya/van, it is considered a roop of Kali. She is wild, uncontrollable, unclothed and drinks blood, and is considered the ugra (angry) or vibhatsa (horrific) roop of Devi. The same Devi, however, becomes Gauri when the reference is to sanskriti or kshetra/sabhyata (civilization). She ties her hair, wears a sari, flowers and ornaments.

Kali's vehicle is an animal of the wild, a tiger, while Gauri has a domestic animal, a cow. The same Devi is both Kali and Gauri.

Who is the god of the van?

The van has many gods—yaksha, rakshas, gandharva, apsara. They are all unconnected with any one place (sthaan). Yakshas keep control over treasures, along rivers or in caves. The word rakshas, according to the Upanishads, has originated from rakshak or protector. Rakshasas protect the forests. In stories, they are always at war with the rishis who want to domesticate the forest by creating a space for their yagnas, while rakshasas reject this parampara. Apsaras are of the water (aps means water), and stay near the rivers. Gandharva means 'of fragrance' (gandha), of plants and flowers.

These are all creatures of the forest, they don't follow any rules. So apsaras never marry; if you try to force them they run away. The Rig Veda tells the story of King Pururava and the apsara Urvashi, in which he (associated with civilization) complains to her (associated with the forest) that she left him when he had wanted to live with her, and asks her to make him a gandharva. This romantic story symbolizes the tension between prakriti and sanskriti.

4

Astik–Nastik

I've heard many interpretations of the word nastik; what is its true meaning?

It is difficult to say what its true meaning is because there are many meanings. It comes from the word asti which means 'aisa hai', or so it is. The meaning of 'it' changes, depending on the school of thought and the historical period.

At one point in time, astik were those who believed (aisa hai) that knowledge could be found only in the Vedas, that is, they were believers of the Vedas, so the nastik were non-believers of the Vedas (who thought knowledge could be obtained from elsewhere too). Later in history, those who believed in karma were considered astik, so nastik were those who did not believe. At another time, there was another group that believed we should follow the path of God, and another that did not.

Usually the word nastik translates into atheist in English—are these terms related?

There's a problem here. The word atheism comes from Europe; it means 'non-believer of theism'. Theism comes from

Theos (God). Here, it refers to the Abrahamic religions—Judaism, Christianity and Islam—where the belief is in one God who created the universe, who also gave certain rules for people which were brought to them by a messiah. If you obey the rules, you'll go to heaven, otherwise, hell.

Words may have different meanings in different contexts, like spirituality and religion. If you say you are religious (dharmic) but also an atheist, in Europe they will not understand it because they believe these are contradictory ideas. All these terms should be considered on their own.

For some, spirituality means that they do not think of the world (bhautik) and worldly matters (laukik) as the only reality, but feel that there's something beyond it; some believe in the atma or the soul, which is beyond the body, beyond the physical world. Some may feel spirituality and psychology are the same—they believe in the mind, in people's hearts.

Tell us about the word secularism.

This word originated in America. It means that the state will be separate from religion; that the laws of the state and those of religion will be kept distinct. Earlier, kings were heads of state and were considered to have been chosen by God. But, with the advent of secularism, the rule of the state could no longer be ordained by religion.

Another definition is respecting and acknowledging all religions and treating them alike. Yet another would be that all religions are problematic and one should keep away from them all—in this, secularism itself becomes like another religion. There is constant debate between these two definitions—is secularism about respecting all religions or being non-religious.

How would you define the term religion?

The word religion is merely 100–200 years old. It was primarily used for Christianity, then for Judaism, then Islam. When it came to India, they started using it for Hinduism. It wasn't used here before that. People would want to know which panth (sect) or sampradaya, parampara (tradition) you were from or what you believed in.

Religion assumes the existence of God, rules, a messiah. Hindu dharma does not have any of these. The concepts of god, rules, heaven and hell are different in various panths and sampradayas. Some people believe in the gramadevata (village deity) or kuldevata (deity of the clan) but not in a paramatma (supreme god). We have so many varieties, that it's hard to use the word religion for them all.

Has India had a tradition of nastikta?

Yes, it's a very long tradition, beginning 4000 years ago. If you look back for the origin of the belief in a god who created the universe, such a concept was first mentioned only 2000 years ago by Krishna in the Gita where he says I created the universe.

The word sanatan means the world has always existed; time and space were always there. We don't need a god, and there is no god who makes rules. The concept of genesis, that first there was nothing, then God arrived and created the universe, does not exist in Sanatan Dharma. At the most it will be said that when god was asleep, there was no naam (name) or roop (form) in the world; only Devi or prakriti. The definition of creation is very different.

Broadly, the believers of the Vedas were called astik and those who didn't were called nastik (Buddhist, Jains,

Charvaks). They did not accord importance to the Brahmins; they claimed to be shramans who would seek the truth by themselves. Among the astik Brahmins too a number of groups emerged. Here, darshan or point of view was important. There were those who believed in logical thinking (nyaya), analytical thinking (sankhya), synthesis (yoga), investigation (vedanta), inquiry (mimansa), etc. According to the Uttar Mimansa, you need to just perform yagnas and follow rituals—that is the truth.

In the Brahma Sutra it is said that the Vedas are apaurusheya. Does that mean they are alaukik (not worldly) or adhyatmic (spiritual)? Rather, it can be said that they are of nature (prakriti) since they are not of purusha (man). So that makes them natural principles. They are without beginning (anadi) or end (anant) because when did nature not exist? According to the Big Bang Theory in science, nothing existed before it—but perhaps they do not know it yet, and will discover it eventually that nature existed before all living beings and will continue to exist after.

The Puranas speak of the Creator, the Sustainer and the Destroyer. These do not mean creator of the world, but creator of sanskriti, culture. Likewise, preserver and destroyer of sanskriti, never prakriti.

In India traditions like Purva Mimamsa, Yoga, Sankhya, Buddhism, Jainism don't give so much importance to the concept of god, so are known as nastik.

What is Charvak?

It's a nastik parampara. Buddhism does not believe in the atma, karma or God, while Jainism believes in the atma, not karma, and has different concepts for God. Charvak does not believe in the atma, God or karma. That which I cannot see or experience, I do not believe in. Only that which I can experience is real, true. This is known as bhautik-vaad or laukik-vaad—materiality or emphasis on the physical world. What is alaukik, non-material, like karma, cannot be measured, and so I cannot believe in it. Charvak is a big parampara in India, but you can't always identify it because it's not a religious school or sampradaya.

In the Ramayana, when Bharata goes to meet Rama in the Chitrakoot forest, he is accompanied by a Charvak called Jabali. Bharata tries to persuade Rama to return to Ayodhya and become king, but Rama refuses, saying he cannot renege on the promise he made to his father. Then Jabali attempts to counter each of Rama's reasons for not returning. He asks Rama, 'Isn't it silly to sacrifice worldly life and live in penury just to fulfil dharma?' When Rama asks what will he say to Yama after his death, Jabali responds, 'Why do you lose the present for what you don't know will happen after you die? What about your responsibility to Ayodhya and its people?' Rama says, 'I want my father's soul to rest in peace and him to be reborn.' Jabali says, 'Who has ever seen the soul? When and how does rebirth happen? Does it even happen?' Rama insists, 'If I don't respect my father, I'll be known as the biggest adharmi.' Jabali replies, 'Man's most significant relationship is with himself. He enters and departs from this world alone. Why do you suffer for someone else's promise? This, now, is the only moment that counts.' Rama is surprised at Jabali's logic and says, 'If I were to listen to you, I'd definitely go to Naraka [underworld].' Jabali says, 'There's nothing beyond this universe. Give importance to what you see; don't waste your intelligence on things outside of that.' Jabali's argument is that there's no soul and no rebirth, so there is no call to torture oneself with these thoughts. What he tells Rama is very practical.

But, according to the astik concept, truth is not merely that which you experience or feel through your senses (indriyan). There's something beyond. For instance, karma is the belief in cause and consequence. Just our experiences do not make up the world. Many things happen which we can neither control nor understand—we can only believe in them. This belief is astikta.

The conversation between Rama and Jabali is a dialogue between astikta and nastikta.

Are Jains also nastik?

The word nastik is often seen as negative to mean that the person does not believe in anything—vishwas-heen. That's not correct. Jainism believes in the atma. Their concept of god is different. God is a perfect being—the Tirthankaras who have found Truth and are in Siddha-loka (the realized world). They are free of karma, their ties to the physical world and they can teach you how to achieve mukti, freedom from this world. So the concept of god here is that of a teacher, one who teaches kaivalya gyan, how to attain liberation, not one who creates the universe.

Those who show you the right path . . .

Not the 'right' path, but the sanatan path—a path which has always been there. You are lost and need to be brought back on it. There's no right or wrong here. If it's not in your karma, you will not find this road now, but after ten births—what's the hurry, the road will remain where it has always been!

Buddhism believes in neither god nor atma, because everything is destructible; it has the concept of unatma. Buddha was once asked about God and how the world was created, to which he gave an illuminating answer. He said, 'If you were shot with a poisoned arrow, would you go looking for the attacker or for a doctor to heal you of the poison spreading in your body? I am the doctor. I am talking of removing the poison that sorrow is. I am giving you a path to relieve you of this sorrow-filled life.'

So, Buddha wasn't interested in theological questions; his focus was practical.

Are you astik or nastik?

In times of sorrow, I am astik, and when things are going well, I become nastik.

In these modern times, people say many different things about their beliefs. What should one ideally follow?

I think people should follow their own system of beliefs, whatever it may be—astik, nastik, secular, religious, spiritual. But also respect everyone for their beliefs. Why control anyone else? That is important. Our country is plural, diverse. We have lot of panths, many dialogues as in Jainism, so respect everyone and all beliefs. Each one has a different karma and thus a different dharma.

5

The Surya Vansh and the Chandra Vansh

I've heard that Rama was a Suryavanshi and Krishna a Chandravanshi, but what are the Surya Vansh and the Chandra Vansh?

In the Puranas, you will always find balance. Like Ganga–Yamuna, Shiva–Vishnu, vairagi–grihasti. To balance the lineages of the kings, there're the Surya Vansh and the Chandra Vansh. At the beginning of each Purana, it is mentioned whether the story is about the Surya Vansh or the Chandra Vansh.

From where did the Surya Vansh begin?

Except for the gods, all Puranic characters originate from Brahma, who is the creator. Brahma is followed by Rishi Kashyapa, Surya, Manu, then Ikshvaku. The word Ikshvaku is related to sugar cane (iksh). Nobody knows why he had this name; a possible explanation is that sugarcane was produced only in India and he was India's king. Everywhere else, sugar was produced from honey (madh). Ikshvaku's descendants are the Suryavanshis.

What about the Chandra Vansh?

The two vanshas are related. Ikshvaku had a brother, Sudhyumna. Once, he goes into the forest where Shiva and Shakti are together. There is a spell on the forest that turns anyone who enters the forest while they are pairing into a female. Thus Sudhyumna becomes Ila, or Ikshvaku's sister. Ila's husband is Budh (Mercury) who is the son of Chandra, the moon god. So, Ila's children are related to the moon and that is the Chandra Vansh.

There's always something odd about the moon. The sun is pratapi, it produces its own light (pratap), while the moon takes it from the sun. All the stories about the moon and its vansh are never clear like the sun. The way the phases of the moon change, these may be hyper-emotional, crooked, where a man becomes a woman, etc.

Ila's story is very interesting—that he was once a man and then a woman.

There are many variations of this story in all the Puranas. In one, it says that during Shukla Pakshya or the phase of the waxing moon, he is a man. And during the phase of the waning moon or Krishna Pakshya, she is a woman. In some versions, he is a man during the Uttarayan, the northern movement of the sun, that is, summer, and a woman during Dakshinayan, the southern movement of the sun (winter). As the year progresses, the gender changes—man, woman or in-between. Ila's story is like that. Her children sometimes call her father, sometimes, mother. Her husband, Budh (Mercury) is said to be neither this nor that. You will find both the categories—both this and that, and neither this nor that.

This has a philosophical meaning as well. You cannot neatly classify everything into boxes. Gender is also a boundary. In the Surya Vansh, there are clear-cut boundaries, like Rama is maryada purushottam, the model man who follows rules. In the Chandra Vansh, there are greys, shadows, the space between black and white. The rules themselves are under question here—what are the rules, how are they to be defined. It's all so fluid that it cannot be said for certain whether you are breaking them or not.

Budh's story is interesting. Brihaspati (Jupiter) had a wife called Tara who did not love her husband as he was a strict rishi. Brihaspati's qualities are associated with Suryavanshis—very rational and straightforward; a somewhat boring husband. She falls in love with Chandra, the moon god, who is emotional and romantic, and elopes with him. An enraged Brihaspati tells Indra to get his wife back. There's a war among the gods and Indra forcibly takes Tara away. When she returns, Tara is pregnant. Chandra claims the child is his, while Brihaspati says it is his. When asked, Tara keeps silent. The child in the womb says, 'I am Chandra's son.' Brihaspati is so angry that he curses the child and says, 'You'll be born napunsak [neuter gender], without genitals.' That child is Budh. So in graphic depictions and idols, Budh is sometimes shown as a man, sometimes as a woman, and he marries Ila, who is a man and a woman. So this is the strange story of the Chandra Vansh.

What is the connection of these vanshas with the Ramayana and the Mahabharata?

The Ramayana is associated with the Surya Vansh and the Mahabharata with the Chandra Vansh. When you say Rama

Rajya, it is associated with the perfection that was embodied by Rama. Kalidasa wrote a long poem called 'Raghuvamsham'. In this, not only is Rama a great king, but so are all the previous kings, his ancestors. For instance, Raghu was a charitable king, associated with artha, wealth. Dilipa who protected his people from invaders was associated with dharma and order. Dashratha's father, Aja, was associated with kama—he loved his wife so much that he passed away soon after her, unable to live without her. All these three qualities are present in Rama. He too loves his wife a lot but is torn between his country and his wife—this is an ongoing tension in the story. Basically, it is about integrity, commitment; one must abide by one's word. Harishchandra sells his wife to keep his word, and Rama abandons his—these extreme behaviours are always found in the Surya Vansh.

Rama was a Suryavanshi and Krishna a Chandravanshi but both are avatars of Vishnu . . .

No one vansh is superior to the other. God does not compare the two or judge them. He'll appear in both. Rama's vansh is straightforward, clear-cut; Krishna's is not. Krishna is leela purushottam. He knows that the people he is dealing with are never going to talk or behave honestly. To deal with a manipulative family, you have to become manipulative. In a straightforward family, you can be straightforward.

Did the Surya Vansh influence Rama or was it the other way round? Did Krishna influence the Chandra Vansh or vice versa? These are interesting questions that can be discussed and are worth thinking over. The admirable thing about our shastras is that they always talk of balance, of one thing complementing another. There's never too much of one thing. Even in our food, sweet and sour are balanced, to bring out the taste. Likewise, the flavour of Bharatvarsha comes from both vanshas.

Are there any stories like Ila's and Budh's in the Surya Vansh?

One of Rama's ancestors, Yuvanashva, has two wives but no children. So he does a yagna, and by mistake he, instead of his wives, drinks the potion from the yagna. As a result, he gets pregnant, and delivers a child from his thigh called Mandhata. So Mandhata's father and mother are the same person.

A very ancient period is often referred to as being 'from Mandhata's time'. In one version of the story, Yuvanashva wonders how he is going to feed the baby since neither he nor his wives can produce milk. There's a belief that gods have milk, not blood, running through their veins. So Indra cuts off his thumb and the baby feeds from it. So, when children suck their thumb, it is a trait said to have come from Mandhata!

Was Manu connected to both these vanshas?

Surya's son is Manu and Manu's children are Ikshvaku and Ila. Today, when we refer to the Manusmriti, we speak of the Dharma-shastra which is recent—about 1500 years old. The Mahabharata and the Ramayana speak of Manu who was the first man. When the British visited India and wished to know who was our equivalent of the Bible's Adam, they found Manu—the founder of both the Surya and Chandra vanshas—and labelled him as India's Adam. And they simplified the Manusmriti as 'Adam's rules', which is not how it really is, because we have so many versions of the same thing here.

Geographically, where are the Suryavanshis and Chandravanshis placed?

There is some speculation about it, and it cannot be proved. The Mahabharata, the story of the Chandra Vansh, supposedly takes place north of the Ganga, Uttar Kuru. Indraprastha is in Delhi, Kurukshetra is in Haryana, Gurgaon or now Gurugram, Panchala is towards Punjab. The story of the Surya Vansh, the Ramayana, is set in the southern part, around Bihar: Ayodhya, Mithila, etc. Rama also travels past the Vindhyas into the Dandaka Aranya, and goes to Lanka in the south. Buddha too is associated with the Surya Vansh, as is Mahavira.

Some believe that the Chandra Vansh is older than the Surya Vansh, but in the Puranas, the Surya Vansh always comes first. It dominated the Treta Yuga, and when I say Bharatvarsha, it is because Bharata was the king and he is a Suryavanshi.

Was there ever a union between the two vanshas, any overlapping or intersection?

Shakuntala's father Vishwamitra was earlier King Kaushik who was a Suryavanshi, and she marries Dushyant who is a Chandravanshi. Another connection is in the Mahabharata. During the great war, Abhimanyu (a Chandravanshi) kills one of Rama's ancestors, Brihadbala (a Suryavanshi). The Puranas mention various lists of lineages, which sometimes cross over, and it can be quite confusing. So one has to see the idea, not the details.

Karna is Surya's son, so was he a Suryavanshi?

Interesting question. In the Ramayana, Sugriva is a Suryaputra, in the Mahabharata, it's Karna. These are separate stories and have no connection with the vanshas. Surya is a Vedic god who may have children apart from the vanshas. So, although Sugriva is a Suryaputra, the main Surya Vansh character in the Ramayana is Rama. In the Mahabharata, Karna is a Suryaputra but the story is of the Chandra Vansh. These concepts cannot be mixed.

Is there any other story of the Chandra Vansh?

Ila's son is Pururava whose son is Nahush. Nahush does so many yagnas that the gods are pleased with him. Once, when Indra has to perform tapasya for some time, he appoints Nahush as temporary king of the gods since he has all the desired qualities. However, Nahush gets carried away and begins to think of all the things in heaven—Chintamani, Kalpataru, Kamadhenu—as his. Even Indra's wife! When he approaches her, she is shocked. To teach him a lesson, she tells him to ask the Sapta Rishi to bring him in his palki (palanquin) to her chambers, as they do for Indra. The Sapta Rishi are horrified at his request, but they agree. One of the rishis is Agastya who is short and walks slowly. Nahush gets impatient and kicks him. Agastya curses him and says that he will roam the earth as a snake and someone from his family will save him and in return he will teach them never to be so conceited. In the Mahabharata, the Pandavas meet Nahush in the forest and he advises them to never become arrogant like him or else they will lose their kingdom.

These negative stories are usually of the Chandra Vansh, but are interesting nevertheless. All the stories in shadow (chhaon) are associated with the Chandra Vansh and stories in light (dhoop) with the Surya Vansh.

6

Atma

What is the exact meaning of atma? Is it soul or mind?

Atma is what makes a being alive—the ability to be conscious. It's not related to time or space. It's anadi (without beginning), anant (endless), nirgun (formless). Any material object can decay with time, is located in a particular space and has certain properties. The opposite of this, that which is unaffected by time, space, form, is called the soul. In Hindi, it's called atma. The word originated from the Rig Veda.

Hinduism believes that everything has atma. Do stones have atma too?

One school believes that wherever you look, there's paramatma. According to this, everything has an atma and atma contains everything. Another school says that there are the ajeev (non-living) and jeevit (living), and the non-living do not have an atma whereas the living do. The inanimate do not have hunger, and are merely made up of the pancha mahabhut, the five basic elements. Where there is atma there is hunger. Plants hunger for water and sunlight, and grow; animals and birds too look for food and water. They are alive and therefore there is fear of death. In this there's an awareness of atma. Human beings have the ability to think, feel with their indriyan (senses); they have a heart and brain. Due to these characteristics, they have an atma. A computer does not have an atma because it does not have a heart or brain, it does not have feelings. However efficient a robot may be, it cannot show you sympathy or empathy; it is nirjeev or ajeev (non-living). But according to the other school, even the nirjeev have an atma.

Do all Indian religions have this concept of atma?

The Rig Veda has an interesting description of the atma. It's actually a metaphor—some say it's a poem—because it's difficult to describe what is formless (nirgun). It talks of one bird watching another bird eating fruit, suggesting that our body that enjoys the pleasures of the world is the fruit-eating bird and the one that watches it is our atma. Our mann (mind) is watching our shareer (body). At one level I am watching you, the fruit-eating bird. On another level, I watch myself. Third level is: Who is observing my mann? That is atma. These are the observer and what is observed.

Observing one's mind is called recursion in English. This ability—of seeing oneself—is present only in human beings. It arises from the atma, by which I can look at (observe) myself and the world around me without emotional attachment or interaction. Our mind feels excitement, happiness, sorrow. The atma is beyond this, separate from these emotions.

In the Upanishads (which were composed 3000 years ago, and came 1000 years after the Vedas), human beings questioned the purpose of their existence—was it just to run after food like all other living things? For bhog? The answer that emerged was that human beings are supposed to look for meaning, for atma-gyan. In Sanskrit, it's called mimansa, that is, inquiry. In science the inquiry is about the outside world, whereas here it is about your inner life. As man went inward, first he saw the flesh, then the indriyan, then the heart (emotions) and mind (rationality). He wondered if there was something beyond this. What is it that is stable (sthir), anant (endless), anadi (has always been there) and is merely watching? The atma.

Buddha did not believe in this concept. He said everything is destructible; nothing is permanent (concept of anicca). Buddhism has unatma or anatta: that there is no atma. What we call consciousness is simply chemistry, for instance, grapes become wine and acquire alcoholic properties. So when the five elements combine, they form both the animate and the inanimate, from where consciousness arises. There's no permanence.

These were the two big schools of thought.

A third school is that of Jains. Jainism looks at the atma as dravya (elements). The world is made up of two things—jeev (living) and ajeev (non-living). Here, they look at atma as that which makes you alive; by which your indriyan are awakened. It is not the same as in Hinduism.

Jainism has a concept of atma whereas Buddhism doesn't?

Yes. Jainism believes that you are stuck on earth (Bhu-loka) because of your karma, which decides whether you will be born on earth or in heaven or hell. A jeev is like a balloon; your karma is the stone weighing it down. The heavier the stone, the further it will sink, to earth, and even beyond to hell. With good deeds the weight is lessened and the balloon can rise, from hell to earth, then to heaven, then to Siddha-loka where the Tirthankaras, the wisest men, are. They do not have any karma. They are completely purified beings.

Hinduism has a similar concept of rebirth?

There are similarities in many of these concepts, but intellectuals will fine-tune them as separate concepts. The Bhagavata Purana will say that atma is god. So you have it, I have it. In Hinduism the concept of jeevatma and para-atma emerges, but we don't realize this because we are ignorant. We are confused and not looking correctly. When we do, we will know that there's god in you and in me. That will liberate us.

There's a story of Gajendramoksha in the Vishnu Purana. This king of elephants is strong and powerful. Once, a crocodile grabs him in a lake. He tries to free himself but is unable to. Finally, he prays to god who comes and frees him. The idea is that god is freeing you from your ignorance that attaches you to things. The bird watching the fruit-eating bird tells her to not be so taken by the fruit and to look at her too. This concept has been described in different ways by different wise people.

What's the difference between jeevatma and paramatma?

Jeevatma is khandit, incomplete, and paramatma is akhand, complete. There are two distinct words—para-atma and paramatma. Para-atma is others. If I don't respect you, it shows that I've become so arrogant that I don't acknowledge your atma, think that you have no atma. If I acknowledge that all livings beings have the same soul inside different bodies, I'm conscious of the para-atma.

When we bring together the entire world's atma, so that it is infinite, that is paramatma; this is akhandit, unbroken, without boundaries. Jeevatma (an individual soul) has boundaries, is caught up in karma. Paramatma is not. Krishna is paramatma, and his gopikas are jeevatma who are seeking completion. A bhakta (jeevatma) seeks god (paramatma); a khandit atma seeks the akhandit atma. In the Aadhyatma Ramayana, Rama is atma, Sita is mann or jeevatma and Ravana, who steals her away, is ahankar (ego) and Hanuman is Bhakti who unites jeevatma with paramatma. These are different stories to bring these concepts to the people.

How do you know whether someone has knowledge of atma? He will not disrespect anyone; he will not compare others; he will refrain from judging. Once when Adi Shankaracharya expounded on atma, people praised him for the wonderful lecture. When he was leaving, a Chandaal (a person who works in a crematorium) approached him. Shankaracharya's disciples asked him to move out of the way—as many people would do even today—for they considered him impure and dirty because he dealt with dead bodies. So the Chandaal asked them, 'Should I move my body or my atma?' Even the Shankaracharya learnt from his.

As long as you are comparing and judging, you do not have knowledge of atma. Relationships of boss–subordinate, etc., are in the everyday, material world. In the spiritual world, whatever differences there may be, all of us have atma. When you don't have that knowledge, feudalism arises, where people are labelled superior or inferior. If you seek meaning or purpose by comparing, and your material wealth goes to your head—like when young men say, 'Don't you know who my father is?'—you do not have knowledge of atma.

Adi Shankaracharya said that jeevatma and paramatma are one and the same—this is the concept of Advaita (no dualism, no division). The Madhavacharya school believed that the two are separate. That jeevatma is the bhakta or devotee and paramatma is god, thus Dvaita (two, separate). Yet another school is about bhed–abhed (separate–whole), which is Vishishtadvaita. It says a tree is paramatma (akhandit) and fruit is jeevatma (khandit). These are different ways of explaining these concepts.

Does the concept of rebirth in Hinduism mean we have another chance or that our atma is trapped?

We can speculate on this and discuss it endlessly, but, broadly, the idea is that how will the atma know about itself when it does not have a heart or sense organs? The atma knows everything but how will it know *itself*? For that, it needs a body. Like we wear clothes, the atma wears a body to experience the world, which in turn gives it self-knowledge. Experience of the world is the knowledge of the hunger that drives a being to food, that instils in her the fear of death, that makes her the bird that looks for the fruit. While running after the fruit, the bhog, she forgets her primary goal. Why am I eating? To stay alive. Why should I stay alive? To experience the world. Why do I want to experience the world? To learn about the atma, which is the primary purpose.

In Kashmir Shaivism, gold is used as a symbol to explain this. We are ornaments made from gold. In one birth you are a bangle, in another, earrings, in a third, a necklace. But in all three forms, births, you are gold which has been broken and moulded into the new shape. The bangle forgets that it's gold and gets excited by its bangle-ness. So this birth, rebirth continues until you recognize the gold (knowledge of atma). We tend to get stuck in artha (material wealth, power) and kama (pleasure) so much that we forget about moksha (liberation).

Would it be right to say that moksha is attained when there's knowledge of atma?

Absolutely. The shramans said that only when you quit worldly matters will you acquire knowledge of atma. But, in the Ramayana and the Mahabharata, they say that you can get it even while doing your daily activities. Rama is happy as a prince in the palace; he is also happy in the jungle. He does not derive his meaning from the palace. He gets it from himself. Sita is happy when she's with Rama. She's happy away from him too because Rama is in her heart. This means they both have atma-gyan.

Krishna too has atma-gyan. He knows that everything is transitory and therefore has no attachment to anybody or anything. He leaves Radha; Dwarka grows and collapses before him yet he remains calm.

Is this concept of aham different from atma, that only when you don't have aham will you get atma-gyan . . . ?

Atma and aham (ego) are in a spectrum. A sheet of paper when crumpled is ahankar. As your atma-gyan increases, the creases in the paper are ironed out, which means aham is moving towards atma. In a term of yoga, Chitta Vritti Nirodha, vritti is the crumple, the knot, of the mind that has to be eased out. If your atma is knotted up like a string, the knots can be opened up only through gyan.

What's the difference between moksha and nirvana?

Nirvana is a word in Buddhism and moksha in Hinduism. Buddhism does not have the concept of atma so nirvana is a release from your identity. Moksha is the release of atma from the material world. To obtain knowledge like the bird observing from the tree.

Christianity has the concept of soul. Are atma and soul one and the same?

Interesting question, because in English atma is often referred to as the soul. Christianity believes in one life, one soul. Here, the soul is corrupted by the Devil. Your soul is polluted because you did not obey God's word as given in the Book of Genesis in the Bible. But there is hope, salvation, in the form of a messiah who will save you, redeem your fallen soul. This concept does not exist in Hinduism. Here, there's rebirth; there's no fallen soul. The soul is always pure and perfect, but covering it is a body that is tied to karma. These are two separate thought processes.

7

Haldi, Kumkum, Chandan, Bhasm

As a child, I remember seeing women throwing red-coloured powder on each other on the last day of Durga Puja. What is its significance?

It's called sindoor khela, which means playing with sindoor, vermilion. In India, sindoor is a symbol of being married (suhaag). This ritual symbolizes the celebration of fertility, the fact that women can bear children, and enjoy grihasta jeevan (life of a householder). Only married women play this game. All these are indicated symbolically in this ritual.

We usually see only men as spiritual leaders. The idea of religion as distancing oneself from the world of illusion and attachment (maya–moh), pulling away from society is known as the Nivritti Marg. But this ritual is of the Pravritti Marg; it celebrates life, grihasti, children, womanhood.

There's another ceremony for married women called haldi–kumkum. Tell us about it.

It's very popular in Maharashtra, Gujarat, Karnataka, Tamil Nadu. Very few religions have festivals of women, by women, for women. Basically, women call other women to their homes, and put haldi and kumkum on each other. It's a home festival where they celebrate each other as in sindoor khela. They'll put haldi, chandan, flowers on each other. Loose hair was associated with freedom. The women have now voluntarily tied their hair for grihasta jeevan, and adorn it with flowers (called 'veni' in Maharashtra). These objects have to be fragrant and colourful. Sometimes Devi, in the form of a pot, is worshipped. A pot is a symbol of womanhood. In the pot is kept a coconut and other symbols of prosperity like betel nut and betel leaf; a house where paan is consumed has success and happiness. So, this festival celebrates grihasta jeevan.

Haldi is yellow turmeric powder, which is an antiseptic; it signifies removing negative energy. In earlier times, women used to bathe with turmeric to give their skin a golden glow. In the Jagannath Temple in Puri, Krishna's sister Subhadra has a yellow face and is called Haldi-mukhi (haldi-faced). The red colour of kumkum is associated with fertility, blood and life. Red is a very shubh, sumangal—auspicious and holy—colour. Mangal or Mars is also associated with the colour red. Mangalya (wellness) in the house is associated with red. In Rajasthan, a bride applies sindoor on her hands and her hand prints are put on the walls of the house. She wears a red bridal dress and walks into the house making red footprints, which too are considered shubh, a sign of Lakshmi entering the house. It may be connected with the redness of the earth. Red earth is fertile, ready to bear a crop (metaphor for children). So haldi is about protection and keeping negative energies out and red is associated with blood, and keeping positive energies in.

Once Hanuman asks Sita about the red mark on her forehead. Sita tells him she is dressing up for her husband who loves the colour red. It is also to signify her prayer for an eternal married life and to ensure her husband has a long life. Hanuman later arrives with sindoor all over his body. When Rama and Sita ask him about it, he tells him about what Sita told him. He says that because she is a devi, a small amount of sindoor will work for her, but he, a mere monkey, has to try harder.

This is a story from the Bhakti parampara where sindoor has been associated with bhakti (complete devotion). The traditional idols of Hanuman are smeared with sindoor. Warriors also used to be covered in red to show their energy (tej or rajas bhav). Over time, this red has changed into saffron (kesar), which is mostly associated with bachelorhood (brahmacharya), which is why Hanuman is mostly seen in saffron; munis, wandering ascetics, Buddhists would wear saffron as well.

When you look at a puja thali, it has elements of many colours. What are the others apart from haldi?

Apart from haldi, there's kumkum (sindoor), abeer which is black, but 'abeer' also means red. There's a white powder and gulal (pink) as well. Colours are important. It's almost as if we are playing Holi with the gods. The colours in a puja thali are to excite the various sense organs (indriyan). Fragrant things (karpoor, chandan) for smell, different colours for the eyes, a bell for sound, prasad for taste, a lamp and its glowing light (deep) for touch. All these offerings suggest the importance of the body. You apply all these on god's body. The atma is important but the atma sits in the chariot of the body. Deha and dehi (body and soul) are both important and must be balanced.

I've seen haldi, chandan and rice being used to welcome a person entering our homes.

It is haldi, kumkum and rice that are applied—in this sequence. Rituals do not have a direct meaning. There's a difference between sign and symbol. Sign has only one meaning. Symbol is yantra in Sanskrit. It can mean many things. You have to reflect on a symbol. Haldi, kumkum and rice can have different meanings. Haldi is associated with male gods. In Maharashtra, in the Khandoba Temple, they throw haldi around everywhere. Kumkum is associated with female gods and you'll find it mostly in temples of Devi. So male and female energy are brought together, and rice is the child that is born. It probably conveys that to grow anything you need two things.

Yellow is also associated with gold, that is, prosperity, and haldi is an antiseptic. Once you remove negative energy and bring in positive energy with kumkum, you get rice, the fruit of labour. In any relationship, the negative energy has to be banished, positive energy brought in, and only then will something come of it. Even in your homes, first you clean the house to keep the negativity out, then decorate it with beautiful things, which is positive energy. Only then do you find peace and happiness.

Chandan is also used a lot. What is its importance?

Chandan and bhasm are to be considered together. Chandan is used more in the Vaishnava parampara (worship of Vishnu), and bhasm in the Shaiva parampara (worship of Shiva). Chandan sticks have to be moistened with water and rubbed on a rough base to produce the paste. The more you rub the more paste you will extract—you have to work for it. While its fragrance is released immediately, you must wait for a while after applying it for the colour to start showing. You have to trust it will be revealed. This is a symbol of karma. Once you work, you will get the fruit of your labour. Don't worry about it; it'll start showing slowly. This concept is associated with the Vaishnava parampara.

Bhasm is produced by burning sticks. Anything you burn is reduced to bhasm (ashes). You don't have to work for it. This gives you an idea of death and mortality. Nothing is permanent. Ultimately, you'll be turned to ash. Shiva, who is a vairagi, smears it all over his body. When he burns Kama (god of pleasure) with his third eye, he reduces him to ash. You'll never know from the ash whether it is of a king's or a pauper's, a sinful person's or a righteous one's. At the Mahakaleshwar Temple in Ujjain, Madhya Pradesh, they use ash from the crematorium in the maha aarti. People these days don't like that practice so they use ash of cow dung (gobar). But, in the Tantra parampara, they'll say that ash is ash, regardless of whether it's from cow dung or a crematorium. Shiva does not differentiate between them since he's a vairagi.

According to the Vaishnava parampara, you must have rules to run a household (ghar-grihasti); there will be the caste (varna) system; there'll be good and bad; you'll keep something inside and something outside the house. There is a belief in hierarchy. Chandan and bhasm are for anointing (uptan), but both send out different messages.

In the Shaiva parampara people apply three horizontal lines on their foreheads while the Vaishnavas apply two vertical lines. What do these signify?

These are pundra or marks. Hinduism is broadly divided into three groups—Shaiva, Vaishnava and Shakta. In the Shakta tradition, haldi and kumkum are used. Parvati puts haldi on her body; she creates Ganesha with it. Kartikeya, her second son, is said to have been born from kumkum. This is related to her fertility, motherhood.

The Vaishnava tradition is associated with chandan—gopi chandan (made of clay) and regular chandan.

The Shaiva tradition is associated with bhasm—gobar (dung) and shamshan (from the crematorium), for the vairagis.

The Vaishnava tradition is associated with action, doing things, living in society. Vishnu takes different avatars, like Rama and Krishna, to accomplish things. To show action, vertical lines are used. As we know from physics, to keep things vertical requires energy. So these vertical lines go upwards, not downwards. There are a couple of reasons for this. Firstly, why is the head important? All life's problems arise from there, as do solutions. Therefore, the head is anointed to remind you that you are human because of it. Invention, ego, all of them arise here. After cremating a body, the head or skull is broken because it's where the atma will depart from the body. In the middle of the lines, a red tilak is applied going upwards (symbol of the material world, or Devi)—almost as if it is being kept in a vertical chandan cup of sorts. Some say this symbolizes Vishnu's feet. What we associate with the sense organs is red, while the atma is depicted through chandan. So the mark symbolizes the balance of the atma and the sense organs; material world with wisdom. That's why Vishnu is called the preserver.

Shiva can destroy all three worlds, so three lines to signify Swarga, Naraka and Bhu-loka. Also, the three bodies in Hinduism—sthul shareer (physical body), sukshma shareer (mental body) and karan shareer (property, made of our karma)—are represented. The lines are horizontal to show death.

Just as there is atma in the body, there's meaning in every ritual.

I've seen people apply tika not only on their foreheads but also on their arms, ears, chest, neck. What does this mean?

Different sampradaya and parampara have different rules. Meanings are different in the north and south, east and west. Broadly, the principle is that all those gods and goddesses we talk about, they exist within us as well. In our arms, throat, ears. So that I can listen to god properly, chandan is applied on the ears. My words (vachan) should be those of god, so it's applied on the throat. I am praying to the god of the throat, ear, hands. Gods and goddesses sit in every part of our body.

Again, we are acknowledging our body—annakosh, or flesh. We are not like the vairagis who smear bhasm, rejecting their bodies altogether to enable themselves to go towards the atma. This is the opposite (viprit) of that. The body has value, it is our atma's chariot. Through this medium, we can experience the world, so we must worship it. Just as we perform god's aarti, we do the same to our body by bathing, applying chandan, sindoor, cosmetics. This is basically to celebrate our body.

8

Hanuman

Hanuman is called by various names—Vayuputra, Anjaniputra, Kesarinandan. Why does he have so many names? What is the story of his birth?

There was a monkey (vanara) called Anjani. Vayu deposits Shiva's seed in her body, in some stories through her ear. As a result, Hanuman is born. Anjani's husband is Kesari, so he is called Kesarinandan. Because he is borne by Anjani, he's also called Anjaniputra. He's born of Shiva's seed so he is Shiva's ansh (of Shiva); and because Vayu brings the seed, his name is also Vayuputra.

There are several stories about Hanuman's birth. In one, Shiva and Parvati took the form of monkeys and Hanuman was born to them.

Is that why many people believe Hanuman to be a form of Shiva?

There is no such mention in the Valmiki Ramayana. Nearly 500 years ago, Tulsidas, in his Ramayana, associated

Hanuman with Shiva. From there many stories originated which connected the two. In some, Hanuman is said to be an avatar of Shiva who is born to help Rama, an avatar of Vishnu. This association could be because Hanuman is a brahmachari. Many Vaishnavas do not like this association. But in the Shaiva parampara, Hanuman is considered Shiva's roop, avatar, son. Different sampradayas and paramparas have different stories about this.

Another story says that Rama and Sita took the form of monkeys and Hanuman was born to them. According to yet another, when Dashratha was performing a yagna, a part of the payas (potion) that emerged from the fire—from which his four sons were born—was taken to Anjani by a bird from which Hanuman was born.

Hanuman was believed to be very naughty as a child. Tell us some of his childhood stories.

Hanuman was very mischievous and unaware of his own strength. There is a famous story about how he thinks the sun is a ber, a fruit, and flies towards it. Surya, scared that the child will swallow him up, invokes the king of the devas. Indra intervenes and stops Hanuman by throwing his powerful Vajra at him. Vayu catches Hanuman midway as he is falling towards earth, and is angry at how his son has been treated. The gods and goddesses ask for his forgiveness and promise to make Hanuman even more powerful. All of them bless him. Concerned that it would be dangerous for Hanuman to have so much power at such a young age, the rishis make it so that he will not know his own power till the right moment; until then he will have no memory of it.

Who was Hanuman's guru?

The god he was trying to catch as a child—Surya—became his guru. Hanuman is a very curious child and is always bursting with many questions. Exasperated, his mother tells him that all his questions can be answered only by Surya because he sees everything. So he goes to Surya and asks him to be his teacher. Surya says that he does not have time since he travels all day from east to west and is tired at night. To that Hanuman offers to fly in front of Surya's chariot, facing him, so that the god can teach him. In some stories, Hanuman asks that if he were to plant one foot in the east and another in the west and faced Surya as he made his journey, could he teach him? Surya asks if he'll be able to withstand the heat of his rays. Hanuman says, one has to undergo hardship to study. Surya is impressed and agrees.

Hanuman learns everything—the Vedas, Puranas, Vedang, etc. He is associated with a lot of knowledge—Sanskrit, grammar, vocabulary, poetry, physics, chemistry, biology, mathematics. At the end of his long education, Hanuman asks Surya what his gurudakshina is. Surya tells Hanuman to always serve and protect his (Surya's) son Sugriva, who is in trouble. That is how the two get associated.

What is this problem that Sugriva is facing?

If you look at the structure of the Ramayana, it's about war and brothers. In Ayodhya, there's tension between Rama and Bharata because Kaikeyi wants her son to be king. In the south, at Kishkinda, the brothers Vali and Sugriva are warring over the kingdom. Their father Raksharaja wants them to share the kingdom equally. But due to a misunderstanding between the brothers, Vali concludes that Sugriva is trying to usurp his share and banishes him. He then establishes his rule over all of Kishkinda. He drives away all the bachelor monkeys and keeps all the women, including Sugriva's wife Ruma, and his own, Tara, for himself.

Sugriva wanders around all alone, having lost everything. Vali wants to kill him, so Sugriva hides on Rishyamukh mountain. This is one mountain which Vali cannot reach, as a rishi had cursed that he would die if he were to step foot on it. Sugriva is trapped on this mountain. This is when Hanuman arrives to serve him. Since he cannot catch Sugriva, Vali decides to torment him. He jumps across the mountain every day and kicks Sugriva in the head. One day, Hanuman catches Vali's foot and threatens to throw him down on the surface of Rishyamukh which will mean certain death for Vali. Vali tries to wrench his foot away from Hanuman's grasp, but to no avail. Finally, Hanuman tells him that he has no personal quarrel with him; he's there only to protect Sugriva. If Vali agrees to leave Sugriva alone, he'll have no problem with him. Saying that, he releases Vali. Vali never goes to the mountain again.

Tell us the story of Rama and Hanuman's first meeting.

Sugriva and Hanuman once see a couple of men walking through the forest. When Sugriva wonders if they're Vali's men, Hanuman decides to find out. Following Sugriva's advice, he disguises himself as a rishi and sits beside the path the men are on. When they encounter each other, Hanuman asks them if they need help. They say that they want to reach the top of Rishyamukh as they have important work there. Hanuman says they seem like royalty and have the bearing of Vishnu and

Mahadeva, and asks why they want to go up the dangerous mountain. A bit annoyed, Lakshmana wants to know why a simple question was being answered with so many counter questions. That's when Rama tells Hanuman that his wife has been abducted and they are looking for her. He introduces himself and his brother, and says that they were told Sugriva would help in their quest. Hanuman is immediately repentant, bows before Rama as his param bhakta (supreme devotee) and asks him for forgiveness.

This story is interesting because Hanuman disguises himself as a rishi, a man. But how is that possible when monkeys have tails? In the Hanuman Chalisa it's mentioned that Hanuman is blessed with ashta siddhi, eight great powers. So he can change his size, fly, walk on water, also change his roop. When he meets Rama, Rama wonders what such a polished man who speaks well, has good vocabulary, etc., is doing in a forest. Hanuman also notices that Rama is no ordinary person. He looks at him with curiosity, is inspired by him. This relationship changes him from an ordinary monkey to Ramadas (servant of Rama), then Mahabali, a supergod. Among the different characters in the Ramayana, you worship Hanuman, but not Lakshmana. Hanuman becomes a god in his own right with temples devoted to him. And it starts with this meeting where he gets his darshan, sees Rama for the first time. It marks the beginning of his growth. So this relationship is very important.

In the Ramayana, there's a chapter called Sundarkand which is about Hanuman's adventures. Tell us about it.

Many Hindus consider it shubh, auspicious, to read the Sundarkand, especially in troubled times. Vishnu's avatar on earth, Rama, also has problems which are solved by none other than Hanuman. He brings hope, changes Rama's story. This has given rise to the belief that when bad times befall you, reading the Sundarkand will alleviate your troubles; Hanuman will solve your problems like he did Rama's.

Hanuman introduces Rama and Lakshmana to Sugriva in the Dandaka Aranya. A friendship is forged, and an agreement is reached. Sugriva does not trust Rama, and asks him to prove his strength. Rama shoots an arrow through seven palm trees and only then does Sugriva accept him with the hope that his strength will be useful against Vali. He tells Rama if he helps him win over Vali, he will help him in return. But after Rama slays Vali, and Sugriva becomes king of the monkeys, he forgets his promise while enjoying life with his wives. An angry Lakshmana comes to kill Sugriva, but Hanuman intervenes and asks for forgiveness, as does Sugriva. At last they go looking for Sita, with Hanuman who forms a search party of monkeys (the vanara sena).

Hanuman's personality emerges in the Sundarkand. As he travels southwards towards Lanka, in search of Sita, we learn of his divine qualities (divya guna) in each of his adventures. One story tells of how he meets a beautiful apsara, Swayamprabha, who gives them food and asks Hanuman to stay back with her. But he is not swayed and turns her down as duty beckons.

The search party is being led by Angad, Sugriva's young son. Hanuman does not have a problem with following a younger and less powerful leader—here you see another of his qualities. In another instance, he doubts whether he'll be able to cross the ocean in one leap. The bear Jambuvan has to reassure and motivate him. So, he comes across as a vulnerable being despite knowing the extent of his powers. Encouraged by Jambuvan, he expands in size like a mountain, his head reaches the skies and he makes the leap. Along the way, he faces hurdles, like rakshasis called Surasa and Simhika. He tricks Surasa by becoming very small and going into her mouth, while he tears Simhika apart. So sometimes he uses guile, sometimes strength (yukti, shakti) to solve his problems.

When he reaches Mainak Parvat, the mountain asks him to rest on him but Hanuman refuses as he's on a mission. In Lanka, he is met by Lankini, the guardian deity, and defeats her. Since he has reached at night and has never met Sita before, he wonders how he will recognize her. He uses his intelligence and thinks there must be something unique about her since she is Rama's wife. He finds a woman in Ashoka Vatika chanting Rama's name. He suspects her to be Sita, but as he's not sure he drops Rama's ring before her. When she picks it up he begins a conversation with her and explains who he is. He demands something as proof to show Rama that he has met her. Sita gives him her chudamani (hairpin jewel) to take back to Rama. Another version says that Sita tells Hanuman a story to take back to Rama. It's a story that only a husband and wife would know.

All these stories show us Hanuman's qualities—foresight, strength, cunning, humility, perseverance, not susceptible to temptation, determination. So they say reading the Sundarkand can hone all these qualities in you.

Then he rejoins Rama and stays with him.

Yes, and he builds a bridge, famously writing Shri Rama on each stone because of which they float on water. He carries a flag with Rama's name on it. He leads the army; they win the war, bring Sita back to Ayodhya, where Hanuman stays with them. He does not associate with Sugriva after this, becoming Ramadas.

In Delhi, people visit the Hanuman temple on Tuesdays, whereas in Mumbai, they visit on Saturdays. Why this difference?

Tuesday or Mangalvar is associated with Mangal (Mars), who symbolizes aggression and war, and is considered Shiva's son. Saturday is Shanivar, the day of Shani, Surya's son. Both are associated with Shiva and to Hanuman since he is Shiva's ansh. So when there is a problem with grahas, Hanuman is worshipped as he is connected with both these days—in some shastras, with Tuesdays and in some with Saturdays. In Mumbai, Hanuman is worshipped primarily on Saturdays, perhaps because the influence of Shani is more there, while in Delhi it is on Tuesdays—the city is known to be aggressive, so that may be the reason for the association with Mangal! Basically, it's become a tradition in these cities over time, and both days are important.

9

Jagannath Temple of Puri

Who is Jagannath of the Jagannath Temple in Puri?

He is the ishta-devata (primary deity) of Odisha. In ancient times, Odisha was known as Purushottam Kshetra because of this famous temple of Bharatvarsha. In the Bhakti period, scholars and poets would visit it during their tirth yatra (pilgrimage).

Is Jagannath a roop of Krishna?

Yes and no. Jagannath means lord of the world (jag—world; nath—lord). Different sects, panths see this god differently. The Vaishnava parampara considers him a roop of Krishna. Some say Krishna is an avatar but Jagannath is an avatari (Vishnu's roop). The Shaiva parampara believes this is a roop of Bhairava; Subhadra is in the centre and on either side of her are Kala (dark) Bhairava and Gora (fair) Bhairava. Buddhists believe this to be an idol of Buddha. Jains believe that the three idols represent Triratna (a fundamental tenet of Jainism). There is a long Jain parampara in Odisha.

Although he's famous the world over as an idol of Krishna, and all sects wish to claim him, in loka parampara (folk tradition), he is bigger than everyone, and so is called Jagannath.

What is the importance of the famous annual rath yatra of Puri?

The temple is world famous because of this ritual. The English word 'juggernaut' has originated from Jagannath. When the British came to India, they saw this huge rath (chariot with many wheels), unlike any they had seen before.

This rath yatra happens in summer when the deity is taken out of the temple because he feels hot inside and wishes to bathe. So, there's a Jagannath snaan yatra where he is bathed in public. Because of this, he gets a fever, so he is kept in the vanasar ghar (recovery room). When he feels better after a few days, he wants to visit his aunt's house, Gundicha Temple, where he goes to enjoy some food. He goes there sitting on the rath, which is the big festival of the rath yatra (journey on a chariot). Huge chariots are built over several months. The rath is made of wood and other organic material; no metal is used. Cloth and beautiful paintings are used. Carpenters, painters, tailors are involved. Many people participate.

In a big ceremony, the deity is brought out of the temple, with his image swaying. The classical dance form of Odissi is said to have been inspired by this movement. The deity's crown too is very grand. He sits on the rath and goes to his aunt's. After a few days he returns to his temple.

This story is associated with many folk tales. When he returns, his wife Lakshmi is upset that he had not taken her with him on the rath, and closes the door on him, refusing to let him enter. To placate her, a bowl of rasgulla is placed at the door. It is believed that the rasgulla originated here, which is controversial because of course Bengalis say it is their sweet!

During the rath yatra, a raja sweeps with a golden jhaadu. What does it signify?

All big Indian temples are closely associated with kings, like Eklingji in Mewar. Most temple rituals are conducted in the presence of the king. Gajapati is the king of Puri. He is considered the earthly incarnation of god. But before Jagannath, even the king is humbled. In our hierarchical caste system, a sweeper is considered a very lowly being. Through this ritual the king himself becomes a sweeper to show his humility. It also shows that god does not consider anyone superior or inferior.

A story goes that many years ago King Purushottam Dev was to marry Princess Padmavati of Kanchi. When her family came to meet him, they saw him sweeping. They felt they could not associate with him and decided to call off the wedding. A war ensued. The king won the war and brought Padmavati as his wife to Puri. He explained to her how we are all equal in god's eyes. So, there's a romantic story attached to this as well.

The broom is golden because a king uses it, and it's for god's chariot. It also shows that though mankind values gold so highly, for god, it's nothing more than a broom.

After the yatra, what happens to the three big chariots that are built?

They are completely destroyed. Nowadays the wheels are bought and sold, but, traditionally, the raths were completely dismantled. This is because everything is perishable (nashwar)—nothing is permanent. In Maharashtra, after Ganpati puja, the idol is immersed in the sea. In Vedic times, after a yagna, the sthal, area where it was performed, was burnt—nothing should last. The following year, the rath is built again, like Ganpati who returns. The idea of continuity and the cyclical nature of things as well as the philosophy of impermanence are represented.

When was this temple built?

In the eleventh century, 1000 years ago, by Chola Ganga Dev. The main temple was built 1000 years ago, but some of the walls around it and some of the artwork were done later. The idol may even be 2000 years old; people of course believe it has always been there. Historians say that the idol was being worshipped as far back as 1500 years ago.

It's a gigantic temple. The iron wheel on its crest is visible from very far away. It was called a white pagoda earlier because it was covered with limestone. When the limestone was scraped off, many carvings were discovered underneath. Some say that the limestone was added to protect it from the sea winds. The temple was very rich, with money, gold and gems, and was attacked often.

Tell us more about these attacks.

In earlier times, people kept gold in temples, not in palaces, because wealth was associated with gods. So invading kings would first attack temples to plunder their wealth. One of the most famous assaults on the temple was by someone called Kalapahad, or 'Black Mountain', an Afghan warrior. According to some folk tales, he was originally a Hindu who converted to Islam, after which he was not allowed inside the temple. Furious, he attacked it. You'll see many walls built around it to protect the temple. These are called Meghnad walls, named after Ravana's son. The area has eight goddess temples (called thakurani). These are the local goddesses who protected the temple like bodyguards. According to another legend a warrior called Raktabahu attacked the temple, and the idols had to be hidden from him. One story says that the idols were dragged outside and burnt but someone saved the dravya (essence) of the idols which they incorporated into the new idols and installed them in the temple again.

The image of Jagannath is very unusual. It seems almost incomplete.

Usually idols are made of stone or metal, but this is a rare temple where they're made of wood. Originally, it is believed, he was a god of the Savara tribe, and maybe that's why the image is different.

There is a story that King Indradyumna wanted to steal the Neel Madhav idol from the tribe. He was a supreme devotee of Vishnu, and Neel Madhav is one of Vishnu's forms. The tribal king Maharaja Vesuvasu's daughter Lalita was married to a man named Vidyapati, an official in King Indradyumna's court. Vidyapati induced Lalita to reveal the location of the idol and told the king. Indradyumna arrived there with his men to take the idol for his own temple, but was confronted by the tribal king. During the skirmish, the idol disappeared.

This story reveals the tension between tribal society and a king from the Hindu set-up, who is building a temple and wants the idol to be placed there. This tension keeps returning in the Sthal Puranas. In the Jagannath Temple too, there are different kinds of Brahmins and pandas (priests). Every year when the god gets fever, Brahmins don't enter. The people who enter are called Daityapati, the pandas who are associated with the Savara tribe.

Is this idol changed every fourteen years?

Yes. Since King Indradyumna did not get the original Neel Madhav statue, he was unhappy. He apologizes to god, and he and his wife Gundicha perform tapasya. God relents and promises to come to them in another form—as a log of wood (daru). They'll find it one day on the seashore, he says. They'll recognize it because it'll be marked with the symbols of shankh, chakra, gada, padma (conch shell, wheel, mace and lotus). They can then carve an idol from it.

When the king eventually comes upon such a log, the wood turns out to be so hard that artisans find it impossible to carve; no tool seems to work. Finally, a maharana, an old veteran craftsman, arrives and agrees to do it on the condition that he'll work behind closed doors and no one will enter till he opens the door himself. Many days pass. Sounds that work is in progress can be heard outside. After some days, the sounds stop but the door does not open. The king feels the old man might have died. The queen tells him not to open the door, but he does. The still unfinished idol was being painted, and upon being disturbed the maharana abandoned his work. This is why the idols are still incomplete.

Another belief is that these are basically tribal gods, like totems. Some believe that the incomplete idols signify that even gods are not perfect; they are like humans. Now that they are on earth, they too are born and will die, like all living beings. Every fourteen years, the god gets such a high fever that he dies. That body goes away and a new body takes its place. A new idol is formed. There's something hidden in the old idol, which is a mystery—some say they're Buddha's relics, because of which Buddhists worship him; some say they're Krishna's bones; some say Shaligram, the fossil that symbolizes Vishnu. Whatever it is, Brahmins cannot even touch it—they cover their hands with cloth, and blindfolded, they transfer this into the new idol. It is akin to prana pratishtha (infusing life into an image to make it god). The old body goes away and a new body comes; the soul moves from one body to another.

The new idols are smaller because they are still children. Each year, as new paint is added to them, they become bigger. It's almost like a living person. All the gods in this temple sing and dance; Jagannath sits on a swing (dol yatra), because he loves to; they go on boat rides; he quarrels with his wife; and even performs the shraddha (last rites) of his parents. All the things that human beings have to do, these gods do.

The Puri temple is associated with eating, and its food is famous. Tell us about it.

Indeed. This is the concept of bhog. In India, there is a parampara of vairagya and grihasta. While the vairagi (ascetic) panths like Buddhism and Jainism withdrew from the world, the grihasta (householder) parampara challenged this. They said the world has been created for bhog (partaking in material life) and consumption. And the gods will show mankind how to do it properly. Bhog is important in all temples as prasad, but here it goes a step further. The world's largest pressure cooker is at the Puri temple. Large quantities of dal, rice, vegetables are cooked, and the bhog is offered every day. There is an Anand Bazaar (market of joy) where food is sold. The message is that bhog, song, dance, beauty, rasa, swaad (taste) are all part of the universe. This Brahmand has to be savoured, and god also does so. He is a part of this cycle, though he knows it will all end. So he is not too attached. The body comes and goes; the rath comes and goes. And yet, he's always beaming.

10

Elephants

Why were elephants considered so important in Puranic times?

In nature, an elephant does not have any enemies. Most animals have a predator that can kill them. An elephant has no such natural enemy. So he roams around without fear. He is large so can go anywhere and find food. The elephant is Goddess Lakshmi's favourite for these reasons. He represents the good life, and has become a symbol of prosperity and happiness. In poems, he has been associated with dharma because he is associated with kings, also artha because he is used in industrial, economic activities (such as for carrying wood and stone, construction of buildings and temples, etc.). Maintaining elephants is expensive so the people who keep them are usually rich. Elephants are also associated with kama or pleasure, desire. A female elephant walking is called gaja gamini, which is also a term for a sexy woman. An elephant is symbolic of happiness, dharma, artha, kama and hence is considered shubh or auspicious.

Tell us about Airavata, the elephant who is Indra's vehicle.

He is a special elephant because he has emerged from the Kshir Sagar, and is white in colour. He has seven trunks, and six pairs of tusks. A Mercedes among elephants! Because he is in the sky, elephants are also associated with clouds—white elephants with white clouds, and black elephants with black clouds from where Indra flashes lightning and brings rain.

In Puranic stories, elephants were flying creatures and used to have four wings. Once, many elephants perched on a tree, forgetting their weight. The tree collapses on the rishis sitting under it and injures them. In anger, they curse the elephants, saying that their wings will be removed. Indra takes away their wings. It is said that an elephant's best friends are still the clouds and when he trumpets loudly, clouds come forth in response. Rain, clouds and elephants have a strong relation. A herd of elephants is associated with monsoon clouds.

Is Lakshmi's vehicle also an elephant?

Yes, what is known as Gaja Lakshmi, but in most images we see a male and female white elephant standing on either side of her—she does not sit on an elephant. White is associated with celestial elephants. It's said that when Lakshmi arose from the Amrita manthan, eight elephants came with her. These elephants, a symbol of clouds, sprayed water on her, did her abhishek (purification, ritual bathing) and welcomed her. Which is exactly what rains do; only when it rains can Lakshmi rise from the earth, and crops grow. In the absence of rain there'll be drought and our agricultural economy will collapse and Lakshmi (wealth) will not come.

Lakshmi's elephants are associated with digga, or directions. There are elephants in all eight directions—four cardinal (north, south, east, west) and four ordinal (north-west, north-east, south-west, south-east). They are called Diggaj—what we now understand as great people. These great elephants stand in the four corners of the world, in pairs (a male and a female), so eight in all. The male is associated with strength, power and the female with sensuality, fertility.

Shiva is called Gajantaka or elephant-slayer. What's the story behind this?

Although elephants mostly carry a positive meaning, sometimes they take negative forms as well. There's an asura called Gaja-asura. Shiva fights him, slays him, tears off his skin and wraps it around his body. The image of Shiva dancing on an elephant's head while holding up its skin is called Gajantaka Murti or Gaja Samhara Murti. Shiva always wears a gaja charma (elephant skin) around his body. An elephant's skin is crumpled, stinky, full of blood and fat, and so it cannot be tanned and used like leather. So someone wearing it presents a horrific (vibhatsa) image. In artwork, Shiva is shown with deer or tiger skin only because it is nicer to paint; artists prefer yellow over black! Shiva is always with gaja charma or vyagra charma (tiger skin), but mostly gaja charma.

This is significant because his son is Ganesha. It is said that Shiva killed this elephant and put his head on Ganesha. Another story says that he cut off Airavata's head to put it on Ganesha. In Bengal and Odisha, a Ganesha idol is always white, symbolizing Airavata. Ganesha, again, is associated with wealth, power, prosperity. Ganesha is a positive image, Gaja-asura is negative.

Symbolically, gaja is associated with worldly aspects of dharma, artha, kama, happiness, and not with moksha. When Shiva is associated with vairagya and moksha, he kills the elephant. But when he becomes a householder, he brings the elephant into his home as Ganesha. So he's accepting worldly aspects.

What's Vishnu's connection with the elephant? I've heard a story where he kills a makar, crocodile, to save an elephant?

Yes, it's the story of Gajendra moksha. One of the oldest images of Vishnu comes from the Deogadh Temple where the wall carvings show Vishnu saving an elephant whose leg is in the vicious grip of a snake, not a crocodile. This is Gajendra, the king of elephants, who is stuck in a lake of lotuses because a snake has its leg in its grasp. It suggests that he's trapped in the world of pleasure (indrajaal) and cannot escape. The fact that Vishnu is saving him suggests one can find release from worldly trappings (samsaric jeevan) by praying to the preserver. So he's giving the elephant mukti, liberation. It's a very important story in the Vaishnava parampara.

In another story, Krishna slays an elephant called Kuvalayapida. In Mathura, Kamsa sends this elephant to attack Krishna, who stops the animal and kills it instead. Krishna then kills Kamsa with the tusk of this elephant.

What is the importance of elephant in Buddhism and Jainism?

These are monastic, ascetic traditions but these too have a place for elephants. All religions in India do. In fact, the first images, carvings of elephants are found in the seals of the Indus Valley civilization. It is believed that when Buddha was in his mother's womb, she dreamt of a white elephant, or of an elephant entering her womb. Dreaming of elephants was considered auspicious, because it meant that something big was going to happen, that an eminent king or a rishi was going to be born. This same concept is seen in Jainism. An elephant dream indicates that a great soul—a tirthankara, a chakravarti, or a vasudeva—will be born. Usually white elephants, or a pair of elephants.

Buddhist thought has another story. Once, when Buddha was walking, his enemies sent a mad elephant towards him to kill him. But the elephant quietened down when he came across Buddha's calm energy. He sat with him and bowed to him instead.

The symbol of the second Jain Tirthankara, Ajitnath, was an elephant, while that of the first, Rishabhnath, was a bull. The Jains too have a Ganesha. They say that Parshvanath, the twenty-third Tirthankara, used to have yaksha and yakshini as guardians. The yaksha is the exact image of Ganesha but rides a turtle instead of a mouse.

In earlier times, while building a Buddhist stupa or Jain and Hindu temples, there were always carvings of elephants. You can see these in the Mukeshwara Temple, Khajuraho Vishwanath Temple, Konark Sun Temple, Cheenakesava Temple, Khajuraho Lakshmana Temple, etc. Some of these depictions are not very pleasant; in fact they are quite violent, either crushing someone or at war. Others are shown singing and dancing. But they are always there as symbols of prosperity, wealth, power.

Are elephants worshipped outside India too?

Interestingly, the elephant has been given importance in the Koran as well. The year Muhammad was born, the king of

Yemen wanted to attack Mecca, break the Kaaba. He was seated atop his white elephant but the elephant refused to enter the city. That was called the Year of the Elephant. In Arab countries too, the elephant is considered auspicious.

Doesn't the Mahabharata have many elephant stories too?

Indeed. The first time the animal appears is in the form of Ganesha who is writing the Mahabharata as Vyasa narrates it to him. So Gajamukha appears at the beginning of the Mahabharata. The most important story is of course that of Ashwatthama, Dronacharya's son. During the great war, the Pandavas plot to get Dronacharya to cast down his weapons. Bhima kills an elephant called Ashwatthama. Yudhishtira tells Drona that Ashwatthama has been slain and that he's not sure whether it's the elephant or his son. Dronacharya becomes upset thinking it must be his son, and drops his weapons.

In Karnataka, there's a folk tale about Kunti and Gandhari. They are believed to be very competitive mothers, not weak and vulnerable as depicted in TV serials! Every year there is an elephant puja in Hastinapur. As the widow of the former king, she can only afford elephants made with mud. When she goes into the palace she finds Gandhari worshipping golden elephants. She feels bad, goes home and cries before her sons. Arjuna is pained and tells her not to worry; he promises her that he'll bring Airavata from his father, Indra. 'You can then worship Airavata himself, which is even better than golden elephants.' But how will he bring the celestial elephant from the heavens, Kunti asks him. Arjuna says he'll build a ramp with his arrows going up to heaven, using which Airavata can come down to earth.

Significantly, the name Hastinapur means City of Elephants. Today, there's no sign of it, but in ancient times, the area near Delhi where Hastinapur was supposed to be was a jungle full of elephants.

Elephants are also associated with important festivals.

In the summer months, elephants are worshipped in many Indian temples so that they will come, be happy and trumpet, thus summoning the monsoon clouds that will bring rain. During the Pooram festival in Kerala all the temple elephants are decorated ornately and brought together on a large ground. Idols of gods and goddesses are placed atop the elephants who are worshipped, given food and sugar cane to please them and make them trumpet.

In Puri, there's a snaan yatra, when the gods and goddess in the Jagannath Temple are brought out and bathed in open air during summer. It is said that at this time they give darshan to their devotees in the form of elephants. The story is that a devotee once says he worships only elephants and refuses to pray to Jagannath since he does not resemble one. So Balaram takes the form of a white elephant and Krishna that of a black one. Such stories are all related to the summer.

In the Konark Temple a lion sits atop an elephant. What's the significance of this?

This motif of a lion on top of an elephant is seen in many temples. An elephant is associated with kama, pleasure. The lion is a symbol of intellect. The intellect must conquer pleasure, or keep it under control. Another explanation of this image is that the elephant is the earth and the lion, a king. This image establishes the king's authority over his kingdom.

I've heard of nagamani and also gajamani. What's a gajamani?

This concept is popular in Indian danta kathas (mythology). Just as there's a nagamani (jewel) on the hood of a naga (serpent), there is a gajamani which is in an elephant's head; it's very rare.

A very rich man once goes to the Puri temple and offers a very large sum of money (say, ten lakh rupees), asking that food worth that amount be offered to the gods. The priests wonder how they can make so much food so they approach Krishna. He says, ask him to give me paan, but the chuna (limestone) on it should be made with gajamani. The rich man gets scared when he hears this, and wants to know what a gajamani is. He is told that one in 10,000 elephants might have this jewel in its head. So he will have to buy all these elephants and kill them to find the gajamani. The rich man realizes that all his wealth will fall short before the sea of eternity.

11

Rama's Ancestors

The word Raghukul is associated with Rama. What does it mean?

It means the 'family of Raghu'. The dynasty of kings (vanshavali), where they have come from, is very important. Not just royalty, traditionally in India, whenever we meet a person we always ask where they are from, their kul, gotra. This is so that we can 'locate' a person, and conduct ourselves appropriately—whether we can sit and talk together, etc.

So when the question arises which tree is Rama the fruit of, the answer is Raghukul. Raghu was a great and illustrious king, the progenitor of his line. He was followed by Aja, then Dashratha who had four sons: Rama, Bharata, Lakshmana, Shatrughna.

Rama is also known as a Suryavanshi. What is the connection of the Surya Vansh with this kul?

There are two main vanshas of kings in India: the Surya Vansh (clan of the sun god) and the Chandra Vansh (clan of the moon god). The Surya Vansh is a big tree; one branch of it was Raghu, another was Rama.

Tell us about the other kings of the Surya Vansh.

First is Manu, then Ikshvaku, then Mandhata. Before our present time, the Kali Yuga, was Krishna's time, and before him was Rama. When you say 'from Mandhata's time', it refers to a time before both Krishna and Rama. Mandhata too is Rama's ancestor. Kalidasa has written a beautiful poem on Rama's recent ancestors called the 'Raghuvamsham'. These are Dilipa, Raghu, Aja, Dashratha and then Rama. The list is not standard. Sometimes Dilipa comes after Raghu, sometimes, before. Broadly, the purpose of this is to show that they came from an important gharana, vansh (lineage).

In Valmiki's Ramayana, during the Baalkand (childhood episode), when Rama is going to Mithila with his guru Rishi Vishwamitra, the rishi tells him about his family. He tells Rama that Ganga came from heaven to earth because of his family, the sea was created because of his family. He wants to show him what an important family he comes from. We learn about Raghukul for the first time in the Ramayana.

Was Manu the first king of the Surya Vansh?

Manu is the progenitor of all human beings. The word comes from mann (mind). Thus all kings originated from Manu. Whoever has mann has originated from Manu—you, me, all of us.

Tell us the story of King Dilipa and Kamadhenu.

Kamadhenu wants Dilipa to protect her, which he promises to do. Once, in the forest, a lion approaches the king and tells him that he wants to eat the cow since he is hungry. Dilipa tells the lion to eat him instead, because he's given his word—the word of Raghukul—and is committed to keeping it.

A deeper, metaphorical meaning of this story is that a cow is a domestic animal, which belongs to a kingdom, and represents artha vyavastha (economy), the world of civilization. A lion is a wild animal, unconnected to civilization. The king stands on the boundary between these two worlds. In the jungle, the instinct is to be aggressive, to dominate; it is where matysa nyaya (law of fish, where bigger fish eat up smaller fish) applies. The king needs to keep the jungle at bay to protect and secure his kingdom. The ability to protect cows (gauraksha) is always expected of kings. Some people take it literally but the metaphorical meaning is more powerful. The first duty of a king is to protect the Kamadhenu and Dilipa did it. Dilipa is associated with dharma.

Tell us the story of Raghu.

Raghu performed the Ashwamedha yagna and conquered the world, becoming a Chakravarti Samrat, an illustrious king. Before going to the forest for vanaprastha ashram, he donated cows among his people (go-daan) and established a strong artha vyavastha in his kingdom. Dilipa protected cows, and Raghu donated them; so Dilipa is associated with dharma, and Raghu with artha.

Raghukul and heaven are closely related because all Raghukul kings become Indra. This is why Indra is always jealous of and insecure about the scions of Raghukul, thinking that someone will come and replace him. In our Puranas, Indra is a position, not one person. So whoever does good work on earth becomes Indra. In the Ramayana, Indra is terrified of the Surya Vansh because most Indras come from this clan, particularly of Sagar who is an ancestor of Rama.

Tell us Sagar's story.

Sagar means ocean, and it was created by King Sagar.

The story goes that Sagar is performing a yagna, his 1000th, and upon its completion he will become the king of heaven. Indra becomes nervous and steals the king's horse and hides it in Kapila Muni's ashram. Sagar asks his sons to find the horse so that he can complete the yagna. They start digging the earth to look for the horse, and end up creating such a deep ditch that when water collects in it, it becomes the ocean. So Sagar's sons are credited with creating the ocean. Finally, at the end of their search, they arrive at Kapila Muni's ashram and accuse him of having stolen the horse. Kapila Muni is doing tapasya and gets very angry at being disturbed; he opens his eyes and reduces all of Sagar's sons to ash.

Devastated by his sons' death, Sagar wonders how to get them back. He prays to the gods who tell him that if the ash is put into the waters of the heavenly river Mandakini (another name for Ganga), they'll be reborn. Thus the concept of rebirth is introduced through this story in the Valmiki Ramayana. But how was the king going to get the river from the heavens to the earth? His grandson Anshuman does tapasya, as does Dilipa, but they do not succeed in this near-impossible task. Finally, Bhagirath, their descendant, is granted a boon that he will be able to bring the river down to earth. Even today, taking up an extremely difficult task is called Bhagirath prayas (effort).

The famous story of the river flowing to earth through Shiva's dreadlocks is also part of this tale. The river comes to earth, Sagar's sons' ashes are submerged in it and they are reborn. Thereafter the river flows into the ocean that Sagar's sons had created. This is how Rama is connected with the ocean, the Ganga and rebirth. Rama's name is chanted during the last rites (Rama naam satya hai) because he is connected with the idea of rebirth. This is not an ordinary story because for the first time, Indian philosophy was conveyed to the people through this medium.

Amidst all these serious stories, are there any romantic stories related with Raghukul?

The most romantic story is that of Rama and Sita, which makes up a major part of the Ramayana, where there are so many complexities. Another story is about Rama's ancestor Aja, which is narrated by Kalidasa in the 'Raghuvamsham'.

Indumati is a beautiful princess who chooses King Aja in a svayamvara and marries him. They are happy and deeply in love. Unfortunately, once, while out on a stroll, the queen is crushed by a falling tree. The king is grief-stricken. He continues to grieve, and finally when their son Dashratha turns fifteen, Aja hands over the throne to him and says he will take sanyas. This is a serious story but also one of the few instances where a husband is shown grieving for his wife. Usually it's the other way around; it is always a woman who is shown in bereavement—viraha dukha. However, Kalidasa frequently shows men pining for women: Dushyant for Shakuntala, Aja for Indumati. Aja's story is so tragic, his grief so intense that he cannot live without his wife. It is not quite sati, but he takes jal samadhi (submerges himself in the sea).

This too is about integrity, albeit within personal relations. The stories of Raghukul are associated with sagar, dharma, artha, kama—it's a glorious family.

What is the story of Bhagirath's birth?

This story is from the Krittivasa Ramayana from Bengal. Since it's not from the original text, it is slightly controversial. King Dilipa has two wives, but no children, so he organizes the Putrakameshti yagna for a child, as Dashratha does too. However, while the yagna is being conducted, Dilipa dies. His widowed wives wonder what to do with the payas, the potion that has emerged from the yagna. They consume it and make love to each other, of which a baby is born. In the Tantric school of thought, it's said that a baby's solid parts, such as the bones, come from the father, and flesh and blood from the mother. Since this child is created by mothers alone, it does not have bones; it's just a lump of flesh and blood. The queens don't know what to do. Sage Ashtavakra comes and blesses the child and it acquires bones. The child is then named Bhagirath ('bhag' is woman and 'rathi' is lovemaking).

This vansh talks a lot about integrity. Are there no negative characters here?

Just as any tree may have some bad fruit, there are a few unsavoury characters here too. In the Puranas, there are recurring stories of the competition between Vishwamitra and Vasishtha; the latter is a devarishi (a rishi from birth), while the former is a king who becomes a rishi. One of Vasishtha's sons, Shakti, was said to have cursed Vishwamitra's son Saudas, that he'd be a cannibal (nara-bhakshi). As a result he would not be able to have relations with his wife. Saudas was a Rahguvanshi, and after the curse people were scared of him.

Another slightly negative character is Trishanku. His name was originally Satyavrata but he commits three big crimes—he kills a cow, eats its flesh and has an adulterous relationship with a married woman—which earns him this new name. As punishment his father drives him away from home. He goes into the forest, does tapasya, and asks to be accepted in heaven. Indra in Swarga-loka says that because he is a sinner, he cannot enter heaven. When Vasishtha refuses to help him, he goes to Vishwamitra, who promises to send him to heaven. But Indra does not want him in Swarga-loka. So Trishanku gets stuck between heaven and earth. To call someone Trishanku is a reference to he who is stuck between two worlds, who belongs neither here nor there. Trishanku is also of the Surya Vansh.

One of my NRI friends calls himself Trishanku; he says he's neither an Indian nor an American, and doesn't belong to any one place.

Whenever we talk of the Surya Vansh and the Chandra Vansh, we talk only of men. Weren't there any women in these vanshas?

If we look at Puranic stories through a modern lens, it's quite depressing because they're dominated by men. Vansh is always seen as male lineage; a king passes his throne to his son, and it continues like that. Historically, there have been queens in India and they have played important roles, but the vansh/lineage is not traced through them. Although the Pandavas are called Kaunteya (the sons of Kunti), they are said to be descendants (vanshaj) of Pandu, not Kunti. This division is always there.

12

Mountains

It is believed that Mount Meru is the centre of the earth. Is this true or is it just a concept?

When it comes to Puranic stories, you have to know whether you are speaking of scientific truth or believed truth. These are concepts, ideas, psychological tools (yantra) to explain some things. Meru means the base foundation. The vertebral column in our body is called merudand (the staff of Meru), our body's centre; if anything goes wrong with this, we will fall seriously ill. Likewise, the world has a centre, its merudand.

A mountain is an important concept in all mythologies and religions of the world. In Greek mythology there's Mount Olympus, and in the Bible there's Mount Sinai from where Moses (Musa in Islam) descended. In the Puranas, Meru has been given a lot of importance. Here, geography has been described poetically. Each petal of a lotus flower in full bloom is a continent and in the centre stands Mount Meru. One of the continents is Jambudweep, in the shape of a jambul fruit; this is Bharat. In Bharatvarsha there are many mountains, but the primary mountain is Meru. Sometimes, Meru is called Mandar, and is associated with the gods. On top of the mountain, near the clouds, is Amravati, abode of the gods. From this mountain originate rivers to irrigate the petals (continents). This is a beautiful, poetic concept.

How are Vishnu and Shiva related to Meru?

This is interesting. As I've mentioned earlier, Shiva is associated with vairagya or asceticism and Vishnu with the worldly life (grihasta). Meru's relation with them is also the same. It is believed that beyond the salty waters around the continents is the Kshir Sagar, the ocean of milk. The asuras and devas used Meru as the churning staff for the Amrita manthan, to extract Amrita from this ocean. So, Vishnu used it for creativity, to produce many precious things useful for the worldly life—dharma (Saranga, Airavata, Ucchaishrava), artha (Kaustubh or the Chintamani, Parijat or Kalpataru, Kamadhenu), kama (Nidradevi, apsara, Chandra, gandharva, varuni).

Shiva's story is quite the opposite. Three asuras once established a place, Tripura (three purs; pur means city). These were three cities of three asuras that were afloat in space, not unlike flying saucers. These asuras would fly off to different places and trouble people as well as the devas. They had Brahma's boon which made it nearly impossible to destroy them. The only way to destroy the cities and the asuras is to do so at once, but with the cities always floating in different directions, never aligning together, it is extremely difficult. So Shiva takes on the task. He says that the moment they are aligned, I will shoot an arrow. But he requires a powerful arrow and bow to do so. He makes Mount Meru the shaft of his bow and the serpent Vasuki the bowstring. Vishnu himself is to be the arrow. But after killing the asuras, he feels so remorseful that he smears the ash from the destroyed cities on his forehead, known as 'tripundra' (three marks) to depict the three cities. These could also be a metaphor for the three worlds—Patala (netherworld), Bhu-loka (earth), Swarga-loka (heaven).

So Meru can be productive with Vishnu and destructive with Shiva.

Why are mountains so important in Puranic stories?

Mountains are symbols of stability. Mountains are there when you are born; they are still there when you die. They are, in a sense, eternal, symbols of immortality. The opposite of this is water (ocean, sea, river), which is never stable. Water has waves; it is always flowing. Vishnu is associated with oceans and Shiva with mountains. There's a balance.

Shiva and Parvati are always associated with mountains. Shiva with Mount Kailasa and Parvati, as her name suggests, is Parvat's (mountain's) daughter.

Meru and Kailasa are very different from each other, and always compete for attention. Meru has flowing rivers, streams, greenery, trees, fruits and flowers; it's fragrant, colourful, rich and fertile. Kailasa is the opposite—it's rocky, snow-covered, still, colourless, lifeless. The gods and their abode, Devlok, are associated with Meru and the vairagi, tapasvi Shiva, with Mount Kailasa. Nothing grows there, but it does not affect Shiva who is always in deep meditation and does not need anything. It's a formidable mountain and people are afraid to go there.

But Shiva, with his knowledge and power, meditating there by himself is of no use to anyone. Indra doesn't dare to go there, so to bring him down from the mountain, the gods pray to Devi. Devi takes birth as Parvati, the daughter of Parvateshwar, god of the mountains. The most supreme of all mountains are the Himalayas and so Parvateshwar is also called Himavan; and Parvati is also known as Haimavati (daughter of the Himalayas). She is also known as Girija, daughter of Giriraj (king of the mountains), and Shailavati, she who is born of the stone (shila).

She convinces Shiva to come down to earth and become a householder, partake in the world. She brings him to Kashi (Varanasi) where the river flows; that is, from the stable (sthir) world to the unstable (asthir) world. The tension between these two worlds constantly plays out in Puranic stories.

We've heard very interesting stories about Krishna and Hanuman both having lifted mountains. Tell us about them.

In the Bhagavata Purana, an angry Indra inflicts heavy showers on Gokul in an attempt to drown and destroy the village. Krishna lifts up Govardhan Parvat on his little finger and uses it as an umbrella for the people. Again, this demonstrates Krishna's strength. Interestingly, it is also believed that Govardhan was made of cow dung (gobar); that it wasn't a natural mountain.

In the Ramayana, during the battle with Ravana, Lakshmana is injured by an arrow. The only thing that can save his life is the Sanjivani herb, which grows on the Gandhamadan Parvat (fragrant mountain) in the north. Hanuman is sent to fetch the herb, but he cannot find it. As time is of the essence, he picks up the entire mountain and brings it to Lanka. This shows his incredible strength.

When Hanuman is flying towards Lanka to find Sita, he has many adventures. He encounters a number of dangers on the way, in the form of asuras and monsters (like Simhika, Surasa). He then comes upon Mainak Parvat. Mainak identifies himself as Himavan's son. He asks Hanuman to rest against him, since he must be tired, and then proceed to Lanka. But Hanuman turns down his help, saying he has no time to rest. Mainak realizes what a great soul Hanuman is. So, Hanuman is called Mahavir, Sankatmochan, someone who will not rest until he has solved your problem. Mainak Parvat is a curious mountain because it rises up from the ocean to offer Hanuman rest, but when he refuses, it sinks back—almost like a mobile mountain!

In another story, Ravana wants to take Shiva to the south where he resides. Shiva agrees, and Ravana picks up Mount Kailasa, arrogantly claiming to have Shiva in his possession. To squash his conceit, Shiva presses his big toe from where he sits on top of the mountain, bringing the mountain crashing down on Ravana. In many Shiva temples, there is an idol called Ravana-anugraha murti. Ravana is squashed under the mountain and is pleading to Shiva for forgiveness. The other idol is of Hanuman holding aloft a mountain. The contrast is between Ravana, who is arrogant and has little devotion (bhakti) and is crushed under the mountain as a result, and Hanuman, the true devotee, who can fly even while carrying a mountain. This is a visual method of explaining what true devotion is.

Are any other mountains mentioned in the Puranas?

There are stories about the Vindhyas.

Vindhya was very conceited, and always quarrelled with the gods, grahas (planets), rivers and rishis. Once, he tells

Surya that he'll grow so tall that the sun god will not be able to cross over to the other side. Worried, the gods go to Rishi Agastya to intervene. Agastya goes to Vindhya Parvat; on seeing him, the mountain bows in respect. The rishi says that this helps me go southward so stay as you are until I return. It is believed that Agastya never returned, and the mountain is still bent over.

Ravana's kingdom, Lanka, is also on a mountain called Trikut Parvat, which is associated with the Vindhyas. Once, Vindhya gets into a wrangle with the wind god, Vayu, who threatens to blow him away. When Vindhya challenges him, Vayu becomes stronger and stronger. So Vindhya takes the help of Shesh Naag; he asks the serpent to wrap his coils around the base and hold on tight. The two strengths balance each other out—one, the movement of Vayu and the other, the stabilizing strength of Shesh Naag. This goes on for a while, until the gods ask them to stop it. On hearing Vishnu's command, Shesh Naag relaxes immediately. Just then, Vayu releases a strong gust of wind and a piece of the Vindhyas breaks off and is swept away into the ocean where it becomes Trikut. On top of this, the kingdom of Lanka is established.

In most of the stories about mountains, a common feature is that mountains are transported from the north to the south through some means, either by being carried or being swept away, and so on.

Many important temples like Vaishnodevi and Tirupati are on mountaintops. Why is that?

Mountains are considered close to the gods, as they reach the skies. People live on earth and gods up in the skies. Mountains connect the two. Towards the end of the Mahabharata, the

Pandavas decide to retire from the world and go towards heaven (Swarga) by climbing a mountain as it is believed that the gates to heaven are there.

It is said that Vishnu came to earth from his heavenly abode and started looking for a place that would remind him of Vaikuntha. The seven mountains at Tirupati reminded him of Shesh Naag, who has seven hoods. Thus the mountain range is known as Sheshachalam (that which looks like Shesha Naag), and the seventh mountain is Venkatachalam. Vishnu on this mountain is called Venkateshwar (god of Tirupati).

Further in the south, Murugan's idol at Palani is on a mountain. In Kerala, Lord Ayyappan is also known as Hari-Hara Suta (son of Vishnu, or Hari, and Shiva, or Hara); his temple is at Sabarimala on a mountain. It is said that those who sit on a mountain are tapasvis. So, Ayyappan, having tied a yogapattam (band) around his legs, sits and does only tapasya there. Vaishnodevi too is a tapasvini; she is not in her role as a wife (Bharya) here.

In south India, all Kartikeya temples are found on mountains. What is the connection?

Kartikeya is Shiva's son. Once the two have a fight and Kartikeya decides to leave Kailasa, and head south. According to the jyotirlingas (local temple legends), Shiva goes after him to persuade him, but Kartikeya keeps going further away. Since there were no mountains in the south, his thoughts kept returning to his mountainous home. His mother Parvati decides to send him a mountain with a demon, Hidimba. Like human mothers pack lunch for their children, goddesses are bound to do something similar, but on a grand scale! This is why Kartikeya is always associated with mountains.

Another story is that when he is warring with Taraka-asura, Taraka's brother Surapadmana assumes the shape of a mountain. Kartikeya shatters the mountain with his lance, splitting it and creating a passage. This shows Kartikeya's immense strength; he broke Mount Krauncha as well. So Kartikeshwara is strongly associated with mountains.

13

Karna

Karna is my favourite character in the Mahabharata, as he is for many. There is perhaps an aura about him that makes him so popular. Tell us about him—how was he born?

There's a princess from the Yadava clan called Kunti, Surasena's daughter given in adoption to Kuntibhoj. She serves Rishi Durvasa who blesses her with a mantra which allows her to summon any deva and beget his child. She can become an instant mother, without waiting for nine months. Sceptical about the mantra's powers, she, in her childish curiosity, decides to test it. She calls Surya and gets a child. The child is special because he is born wearing a kavach (armour) and kundala (gold earrings). At first she is excited, but then she realizes that having a child while still a maiden would destroy her reputation. She places the child in a basket and floats it down a river.

Who brings up Karna?

The basket floats to Hastinapur and gets stuck on the bank of the river where sarathis (charioteers) stop to let their horses drink water. A charioteer named Adhirath discovers the baby and takes it to his wife, who finds it beautiful and decides to raise it even though she has children of her own. So this princely child with a princess for a mother and a powerful deva for a father is raised by charioteers who are of the Suta caste, that is, Shudras.

This is where the story of the caste system (varna vyavastha) comes into play. Through the story of Karna you see the hierarchy (samant-vaad) in society. Rathi is the person who sits in the chariot and is of a higher caste; sarathi is a low-caste charioteer who serves the rathi as his dasa (servant). Karna is born a rathi but he is raised by a sarathi. Societal rules at the time demanded that the son take up the profession of his father. Thus Karna ought to become a sarathi. However, to Adhirath's surprise, he wants to become a rathi. He has the attributes of his Kshatriya varna—the desire to dominate, control, fight, to be a warrior—and is adamant on learning the art of battle.

So he goes to Dronacharya, who is Hastinapur's rajguru, and who trains the Kauravas and the Pandavas. The strict professorial Dronacharya refuses, saying he only teaches children of royalty. So Karna goes off to Parashurama, who does not like Kshatriyas and teaches only Brahmins. Karna dresses up as a Brahmin and approaches Parashurama, and learns from him through deceit. One day, Parashurama discovers that Karna is not a Brahmin. He curses the warrior, saying that the day Karna needs his knowledge the most, to save himself, he will forget everything he's learnt from Parashurama, and die.

Whom does Karna marry?

In the Sanskrit Mahabharata, it is not clearly mentioned. In folklore, it's said that he married Vrishali, another charioteer's daughter, a woman from his own jati. But the interesting story is when he goes to participate in Draupadi's svayamvara. Technically, he can win and marry Draupadi. But when Draupadi comes to know his jati, his father and family, she rejects him. Krishna too is present there but he does not participate in the svayamvara. Why he does not hasn't been explained in the text. My hypothesis is that when he watches Karna, a charioteer's son, being turned away, he questions how he, a cowherd's son, can take part. His story, after all, is similar to Karna's; although royalty, he has been adopted and raised by cowherds. In a way, by rejecting Karna, Draupadi rejects Krishna.

There is a story involving Duryodhana in which a different shade of his character emerges. At what could be called their graduation ceremony, Dronacharya wants to exhibit all the skills of warfare the royal children have learnt from him. For the first time, Karna comes into the arena, and says he wishes to participate. Everybody, including Dronacharya and Bhishma, refuses him because he is a charioteer's son. Bhima also insults him, and calls him a servant, unaware that he is his brother (both being Kunti's sons). Arjuna too feels insecure as Karna appears to be his competition in archery. As Kunti watches this drama unfold, she recognizes Karna from his gold armour, and is aggrieved to see her eldest son being insulted by her younger sons. Only Duryodhana supports Karna, saying that merit is important. One wonders whether Duryodhana is actually advocating for Karna or if he is just making the most of the opportunity to defeat the hated Pandavas. Does he genuinely like Karna? He claims he is his friend, makes him king of Anga, by virtue of which Karna is called Angaraj. However, people say that it doesn't change his birth as a Shudra.

This complexity is a theme of the Mahabharata. Karna has a friend who's not a friend, a mother who's not a mother, brothers who are not his brothers . . . This loneliness follows him throughout his life.

Karna is known as Daanvir, an extremely generous person. He is even compared with Harishchandra. Are there any stories about this?

Indeed, Karna is very generous. When he becomes king of Anga, is rich, and is no longer a sarathi—he has become a rathi—he declares that nobody will return empty-handed from his house. Once, a man comes asking for logs of chandan (sandalwood). Karna doesn't have any but his house is made of chandan so he breaks it down and gives the wood to him. In Andhra Pradesh, there's a famous story which tells of a girl who is standing on the side of the road, drinking milk. When Karna drives past in his chariot, her pot accidentally falls from her hand and the milk spills. She starts crying, telling him to return the milk to her. Karna picks up the mud and with his incredible strength squeezes the milk out of it and gives it to her. Though the little girl is pleased, Bhudevi is unhappy; she accuses him of snatching away milk that rightfully belonged to her. She curses Karna and says that one day she too will hold back his chariot so that he cannot move, and that's the day he'll die. Despite his generosity, Karna is cursed. When he's dying, Krishna goes to him disguised as a Brahmin and asks if he has anything he can give him. Karna pulls out his golden teeth and hands them to him. When Krishna comes back for more, Karna says I give you all my punya (good karma that's accumulated). He keeps giving daan so is called Daanvir Karna.

It is said that Draupadi was in love with Karna—is that true?

This is a loka katha (folk tale); it does not exist in the Sanskrit epic. In Maharashtra, there's a famous poem called 'Jambul Akhyan'. Once Draupadi picks a jambul (jamun) fruit. A rishi, who is close by, claims that he had been eyeing that fruit and was about to pick it when she did. He is about to curse her, so she pleads with him. He tells her that if she can attach the fruit back on the tree, he won't curse her. When she asks how it is possible, the rishi says that if she reveals her deepest secret, the fruit will attach itself. Draupadi then confesses, 'Although I have five husbands, I have a special feeling for Karna.' People say she has a 'loose character', but the rishi (believed to be Krishna) says that only a person who can eat a jambul fruit and not get a purple stain on their mouth can claim to be absolutely pure. So, don't judge Draupadi.

At Draupadi's vastraharan (disrobing), the Pandavas, Kauravas and Karna were present. What was Karna's reaction?

One would expect that Karna, having suffered so much humiliation, and being a hero-like character, would defend someone being insulted in public. But Karna does not come to Draupadi's aid. Instead, he calls her a public woman. Because she has five husbands, he says, she can be treated as an object for gambling. It's a very dark sentence. At that time you don't like Karna much.

Tell us the story of Karna's kavach and kundala (armour and earrings).

He has them from birth, a sign of his royal and warrior qualities. Despite this, Dronacharya refuses to teach him.

When he becomes powerful on his own, Indra becomes insecure. Arjuna is Indra's son and he thinks that if there's ever a battle between Arjuna and Karna, the latter's kavach will protect him from Arjuna's arrows. He disguises himself as a poor Brahmin and approaches Karna and asks for his kavach and kundala as daan. Though they are stuck to his body, Karna cuts them off and gives them to Indra. The king of devas is impressed and feels bad about deceiving him, so he gives Karna an astra (weapon) and tells him that no matter whom he aims it at, it will unfailingly meet its target. Karna says he'll definitely use it against Arjuna, which again leaves Indra doubting what he's done.

What was Karna's role in Kurukshetra?

Three men assumed leadership of the Kaurava army as its commander (maharathi)—Bhishma, Drona and Karna. When Bhishma becomes the maharathi, he does not allow Karna to fight in the battle because he is a Sutaputra and because Bhishma holds Karna responsible for the battle taking place. Typically, he was blaming someone outside the family for the feud, claiming that Karna had been a bad influence on Duryodhana, and so on. It's said that Bhishma did this on purpose because he knew Karna was Kunti's son and the Pandavas' older brother.

When did Karna find out the truth of his birth?

Before the war, when negotiations are on to make peace, Krishna goes to him and tells him that he is Kunti's firstborn son. If they were to publicly declare this, by law Karna would be a Pandava. Kunti's husband was Pandu so he would get his rightful share of the property and claim to the throne of

Hastinapur. The Pandavas who had insulted him all along would sit at his feet and their wife would become his, too, his patrani (foremost queen). He would get everything. But Karna declines, saying he will stay loyal to his friend Duryodhana. When he becomes a maharathi, Kunti comes to him and pleads with him not to wage war against his brothers. She tells him that she is his mother. It's a beautiful conversation. Rabindranath Tagore has written a significant poem on this exchange, 'Kunti–Karna Samvaad'.

When Kunti asks Karna to promise her that he will not kill any of his brothers, Karna says, 'I've already given away my kavach and kundala to Indra, I've been cursed by Bhudevi and Parashurama, now you handicap me further with this request. I promise you that except Arjuna I will not kill any of your sons. If I die, Arjuna will live, and if Arjuna dies, I shall live. No matter what the outcome of the war is, the number of your sons will remain the same.' Perhaps Kunti is being opportunistic here, as Duryodhana was before. This is the tragedy of Karna's life.

In Kurukshetra, in the middle of battle, Karna's chariot gets stuck in the mud, as Bhudevi holds it down. He knows a mantra that Parashurama had taught him to get out of such a situation, but cannot remember it because of Parashurama's curse. So he climbs down from the chariot to dislodge the wheel. He is unarmed. At that moment, Krishna tells Arjuna to shoot him with his arrow. Arjuna protests, saying that he is unarmed, but Krishna says, it does not matter, kill him.

I read in your book that Karna went to Naraka. Why so?

The ending of the Mahabharata is interesting. The Pandavas go to hell and the Kauravas go to heaven. But Karna does not. He stays in hell. Those who operated within the bounds of their jati-dharma (caste dharma) in Kurukshetra go to heaven. The Kauravas, as Kshatriyas, stayed true to their jati-dharma, and went to heaven. Karna behaved like a Kshatriya although he was a sarathi. Here, the question of caste comes up again.

Another reason is his breaking his promise to Duryodhana that he would kill the Pandavas. But even though he gets opportunities to kill Yudhishtira, Bhima, Nakula and Sahadeva, he does not use them because of his promise to Kunti. He does not keep his word to Duryodhana, and so goes to hell.

14

Years in Exile

Why were the Pandavas sent into exile (vanavas)?

The Pandavas bet their kingdom, Indraprastha, in a game of dice and lose. The agreement is that in the thirteen years of their exile in the forest, the Kauravas would rule that kingdom. Of the thirteen years, they were to live twelve years in vanavas and one year in agyatvas (in disguise). And if they were recognized and found out in the thirteenth year they would have to go back into exile for another thirteen years.

What did these princes, so used to the luxuries of royal life, do in the forest for so many years?

The Pandavas talk to Krishna and tell him that they could wage war right away and get their kingdom back, instead of going into exile. But Krishna cautions them against that and says they must keep their word, having entered into an agreement. When they wonder what they'll do, Krishna advises them to meet all the rishis in the forest one by one and turn this into an opportunity to expand their knowledge. Learn from the aranyakas (books written by rishis in forests) about the Upanishads, the sadhana (meditation) of the rishis, and so on. All that knowledge would help them become better kings on returning from exile. So they meet rishis who impart their knowledge and tell them stories, go on tirth yatras (pilgrimages), travel to the mountains and across rivers. The third chapter of the Mahabharata is the Vana Parva, literally, the forest of stories, where they are told innumerable stories. This is the core of vanaprastha—kahani, gyan, tirth yatra.

What did Bhima learn in agyatvas?

Bhima is a strong and capable prince, but he is also proud and arrogant. He needed to learn humility. Many incidents take place in the jungle that teach him the value of humility. Once, Draupadi sees a golden-petalled lotus and brightens up for the first time after the vastraharan; she's been angry and upset ever since. Seeing her happy, Bhima offers to bring her more such flowers. He decides that no one will come in his way, and that he will not go around anything; they will have to move aside because he is a prince. He meets Hanuman, who is lying on the ground disguised as an old monkey. Hanuman says he's too old to move and asks Bhima to go around him or move his tail aside. Bhima kicks his tail but it does not budge; he tries to move it with his hands, but no matter how hard he tries it feels like something made of the heaviest iron. This is a famous story, and in the ensuing dialogue, Hanuman tells him that this very conceit is what caused him to lose his kingdom and that he'll have to learn about humility in the jungle.

What is Arjuna's story?

Arjuna is very upset about losing his kingdom, having to suffer his wife's humiliation. He is frustrated and impatient because Krishna has forbidden them to go to war. He does a tapasya to obtain a weapon—the Pashupatastra—from Shiva. While he's meditating, Shiva comes to him as Kirat, a tribal. Arjuna treats him like an inferior person. Kirat tells him that he may have been a prince in his palace, but in the jungle, he was like everyone else; they were equal. Arjuna doesn't agree and they have an archery contest in which he is defeated. Like Bhima, Arjuna too is taught a lesson in humility. Unlike most stories where the hero is shown as being perfect, the Mahabharata shows their flaws.

Then Arjuna goes to heaven to meet his father Indra. There a beautiful apsara named Urvashi sees him and is attracted to him. When Arjuna turns her down saying she was the wife of his ancestor, Pururava, and therefore like a mother to him, she tells him that his human rules don't apply to her. He still refuses her, so she curses him and says that he'll become a napunsak (eunuch). Scared, Arjuna runs to Indra who says he can only mitigate the curse by making it applicable for just one year, and suggests that he use it to his advantage during the agyatvas.

Arjuna is portrayed as something of a ladies' man, a womanizer. This incident perhaps takes place to make him question his masculinity. He pursues women, but has he tried to understand their needs, seen the world from their point of view? When he lives like half a woman for a year, without his masculinity, he'll be able to see the world from their perspective. Again, this is to teach him humility, a kind of mental retraining so that he'll become a better king when he returns.

What is Yudhishtira's story?

The Pandavas meet many rishis in the forest, including Mudgala and Markandeya. When Yudhishtira is moping about the injustice of having to suffer vanavas, Rishi Markandeya asks him why he's sulking when it was he who brought this hardship upon his family and himself. The rishi then tells him the story of the Ramayana, called Ramopokhyan, and how Rama, though completely blameless, happily chose vanavas only to help his father keep his word.

This is another story where the Ramayana and Mahabharata intersect.

Yes, this is told as history to the Pandavas. The events of the Ramayana take place in an earlier epoch, the Treta Yuga, and those of the Mahabharata in the Dvapara Yuga. The story is important to compare their respective vanavas. Their reasons, attitude, approach are different. Rama is forced into exile for fourteen years although he is innocent, unlike the Pandavas who are not innocent, have lost in gambling, and go to vanavas for thirteen years. The Pandavas keep complaining about it, thinking of ways to hurt the Kauravas, whereas Rama accepts it gracefully. Rama in Ayodhya and Rama in the forest are the same—at peace—that is why Rama is god and the Pandavas are not.

There is another interesting, very famous, story about Yudhishtira, Nakula and Sahadeva. It's called Yaksha Prashna. Once the Pandavas feel extremely thirsty, so they ask Nakula and Sahadeva to look for water. When, even after a long time, they don't return Arjuna goes in search of them. He too does not return. Then Bhima goes to look for them and does not return either. Finally, Yudhishtira goes and finds his brothers lying dead near a lake. Since he is really thirsty, he decides to first drink some water and then investigate what has happened to his brothers. A crane in the lake stops him and says, 'You have to answer my questions before drinking the water. Your brothers did not obey me, so I killed them.' Yudhishtira agrees.

The crane asks him, 'What is the most mysterious thing in the world?' Yudhishtira replies that although people die every day, those who are alive behave as if they are immortal. The crane, which is a yaksha, asks him many such questions after which it is satisfied and allows him to drink the water. Happy with Yudhishtira's answers, the crane offers to bring back to life any one of his brothers. Yudhishtira asks for Nakula. The crane is surprised by this choice and reminds him that he has a battle to win. Why not choose the strong Bhima or the archery expert (dhanurdhar) Arjuna? Why Nakula, who is just handsome, talks to birds, and is perhaps of no use? Yudhishtira says that his father had two wives. He, a son of Kunti, is alive. One of Madri's sons should also live. Here, you see the transformation that has come about in Yudhishtira. In the Sabha Parva, when they are gambling, Yudhishtira first bets Nakula (a son of Madri)—the brother who is least close to him. He considered Bhima and Arjuna apne (his own) and Nakula and Sahadeva paraye (someone else's). The realization that a king must consider even the distant ones as his own comes to him in the jungle. This shows that he is ready to become king.

What does Draupadi learn?

Draupadi hears many stories in the jungle. One is of Nala and Damayanti. Nala is a handsome, worthy king and, like the Pandavas, gambles away his kingdom. Depressed, he goes to the jungle; his wife accompanies him. He is so miserable that he runs away from his wife. Left alone in the forest, Damayanti learns to survive, but does not abandon her husband. She believes he will return and keeps looking for him. Finally she finds him, a broken man. This story teaches Draupadi that her support is necessary for her husbands' survival. They were drowning and she is the boat due to which they survive. The wife is given a lot of importance in the Vana Parva. She is the solution, the support, without whom the men can do nothing. Damayanti is strong and supports a husband who is a weakling. She faces terrible situations with equanimity. She even has to become a dasi (servant), under the name Sairandhri, a name that Draupadi also takes later. Damayanti becomes a role model for Draupadi.

What happens in agyatvas, the last year of the exile?

It's interesting from a psychological point of view. The Ramayana and the Mahabharata are stories of kings and queens, and of rishis, where servants are always in the background, almost invisible. In the final year of their exile, the Pandavas assume the roles of servants. For the first time they experience what it's like to be servants (sevaks). Bhima becomes a cook. Someone who loves food has to serve everyone else before eating. He has to learn to attend to others first. Arjuna who was a handsome archer and womanizer becomes a eunuch, Brihannala, and teaches girls how to dance. Nakula and Sahadeva become caretakers of cows and horses. Draupadi becomes a ladies' maid, a hairdresser. Someone who was a patrani now has to do up another queen's hair.

Yudhishtira's tale is very entertaining. He is known for and takes pride in always being honest. He comes as a Brahmin and becomes the king's companion. The king loves to gamble and Yudhishtira plays with him. He also gives the king good advice. Once, the king proudly tells Yudhishtira how his son, Prince Uttar, defeated the Kauravas in battle. Yudhishtira says that perhaps Brihannala, who had accompanied the prince, supported him. He knows that the young Uttar cannot possibly have done it on his own, and Arjuna as Brihannala must have helped him. The king reiterates that it was his son, and again Yudhishtira insists on taking Brihannala's name. The king insists it was Uttar, and when Yudhishtira is about to repeat his statement, the king slaps him, saying, 'Will you not allow me the pleasure of this little lie? Why do you have to be such a stickler for the truth? Do I not know that my son is not capable of defeating the Kauravas?' Yudhishtira learns then that servants are not free to speak the truth. He understands what is called sabhachaturya (tactfulness in court); in the presence of a king or authority figure, you cannot speak the truth.

In those days, there must have been no farming in the forests where the Pandavas lived. What did they eat? Did they hunt?

These days people become very anxious, and hark back to 'those ancient times' when, apparently, non-vegetarian food wasn't consumed. The Pandavas were Kshatriyas, and they hunted and ate all kinds of food. According to one story, they were so bored and tired of listening to stories and doing tirth yatras that they started hunting a lot. Once, Yudhishtira dreams of a herd of deer who tell him to go away from there, because their numbers are dwindling; they will become extinct if the brothers continue to hunt this way. It's a message of ecological/environmental concern conveyed through this story.

15

Vedic Gods and Goddesses

I've heard that there were thirty-three gods and goddesses in Vedic times.

The number thirty-three is used often. In fact, it's also used in Buddhist mythology. It is said that Indra sits in heaven which has thirty-three gods and goddesses. So the number thirty-three is important. Here, there are twelve Adityas; this comes from the word Aditi, and is the name of the gods, and of the sun. Then there are eight Vasus associated with earth, and eleven Maruts who are associated with Vayu, with storms. Maruti is one of Hanuman's names, and Vayu is Hanuman's father. Then there are two Ashvini Kumars—in the Mahabharata they are the fathers of Nakula and Sahadeva. These are the thirty-three gods—some we are familiar with, some we are not. These gods are usually invoked (avahan). The Adityas—sun, Vasus—earth, Maruts—wind, Ashvini Kumars—morning and evening stars.

Who are these thirty-three gods?

In Vedic times, 3000 to 4000 years ago, people performed yagnas which did not have an idol (nirakaar). Gods and goddesses were described in words, through mantras, but they had no form. The Vedas talk of three worlds—Bhu-loka (earth), Swarga-loka or the sky (the celestial realm) that has stars, planets, galaxies, and the space in between these is Antariksh or atmosphere. So probably these are gods of nature. The most popular Vedic god is Indra. Second is Agni, then Som (associated with plants, vanaspati, and the juice therein, soma rasa), Vayu, Mitra, Varun, etc.

Any goddesses?

There are goddesses, but very few. There is Usha—dawn, Prithvi—earth, Aranyani—forest, Aditi—mother of the devas, Vagadevi—associated with speech and language (like Saraswati). Vedas place a lot of importance on language. In fact, Vedang refers to etymology (nirukth), grammar (vyakaran), metre (chhand). These are all parts of language which people associate with Saraswati, although Saraswati is mentioned as a river in the Vedas. Some scholars believe that to be a metaphor for the 'river of knowledge'.

In texts called Brahmanas, where yagnas are described, you'll find many stories. One such refers to the rakshasi Dirghajeevi who has a long tongue and steals the soma rasa from the gods. People say that perhaps this same Dirghajeevi became Kali over time. This is all speculation of course.

Do the gods mentioned in the Puranas find a different shape and form in the Vedas?

They don't have a form at all in the Vedas. They are nirakaar. There are many descriptions: they are strong, powerful, etc.

In the Puranas, we form an image of Shiva as digambara (sky-clad), ash-smeared, wearing elephant skin; Vishnu wears pitambar (saffron robes), is smeared with chandan, and wears a vyjayantimala (marigold garland). These visual cues are absent in the Vedas. It's all abstract in the Vedas, whereas in the Puranas, it's concrete, refers to form and has stories. In the Vedas, characters, rather than stories, are important. You can say the Vedas are the seed and the Puranas, the fruit; the seed gives rise to the tree which bears the fruit. The distance between the seed and fruit is the distance between the Vedic and Puranic gods and goddesses.

Who are the most famous gods of the Vedas?

There are 1000 poems in the Vedas called Sukta. Of these, a quarter are devoted to Indra, described as great, brave, virile, one who solves problems, goes to war, kills vrit (snake), brings rains, releases water, frees cows. However, in the Puranas, he is Brahma's son, insecure, always afraid that someone—rakshasa or asura—will steal his wealth, or that some rishi will take away his position by doing tapasya. He is envious of kings too, and lives hedonistically among the apsaras. So he is not worshipped, there are no temples devoted to him. But in the Vedas, it was his name that was always chanted in mantra after mantra. So it's a big shift that occurred between the two ages.

Isn't there any Indra story in the Vedas?

There are some but not as many as in the Puranas. There's one famous story. A woman called Apala develops a skin disease that makes her look ugly. Her husband orders her to return to her parents since he cannot bear the sight of her any more. As she is walking through the forest, she breaks off some twigs and stops to chew on one. A man appears and asks whether it's from a soma tree and what the juice is like. When she says it's good, he asks her where she found the tree. She offers to take him there. On the way, when he asks her if she knows who he is, she says that she's heard Indra deva likes soma rasa a lot so he must be him. She then tells him that despite her father's reverence and sacrifices to Indra, there had not been a drop of rain in their fields. When they reach the soma tree, Indra helps himself to soma rasa and is pleased. He tells her that from the next day, her father's farm will not be dry; then he cures her disease and disappears. This story tells of Indra's great fondness for soma rasa, so much so that even if you accidentally find it, Indra shows up.

In Puranic times, gradually the word becomes a god's name. So even if you accidentally take his name, all your sins will be forgiven. There's the story of Ajmil, a gambler, who angrily calls his son whose name is Narayan. Just by uttering a god's name, he is freed of his sins and is admitted to Vaikuntha. Accidental fortune, one can say. Apala, Ajmil, both find accidental fortune. The Vedic story is presented in another form in the Puranas. The basic bhav or arth, called nirguni—the meaning, is the same in both. The body (shareer) has changed, but the atma is the same.

In the Puranas, Varuna is the god of the oceans. Is he the same in the Vedas?

In the Puranas, he is the god of the oceans; he is also Lakshmi's father and is associated with generosity. In the Vedas, the gods Varuna and Mitra are associated with morality. Varuna has many eyes with which he sees the world from all sides;

observing whether everyone is working properly or not. Mitra is the god of contracts, associated with ethics, relationships, whether friendly or official. Mitra was a famous god in Europe and was associated with the sun. Idols have been found, as far back as ancient Roman times, of Mitra sacrificing a bull. Apparently, such was his importance at one time in the Roman Empire that if Christianity had not happened, Mitra would have been as popular as Christ. Christianity gives importance to Sunday which is Mitra's day, since he is associated with the sun. These relationships with the sun found in the Vedas are found in Europe too. So there was some connection between the two 4000 years ago.

Today, Western scholars claim that influence flowed from West to East, and Indian scholars say the opposite. This is an ongoing debate, and nobody knows the answer.

Tell us about Agni.

Agni is the second most important god in the Vedas. Indra is associated with water and Agni, with fire, both key elements for a civilization to be established. In modern times, one would say electricity instead of fire. In Vedic times too, fire and water were essential for life so these gods were important. Indra was invoked for rain and Agni was placed in a kund around which yagnas were performed. It is believed to be the mouth of the gods. When you put ghee in the fire and say 'swaha', the food reaches the gods. During a yagna, first the yajman (patron of the yagna) is identified. For instance, I, Devdutt, am performing the yagna, and while chanting a mantra for Indra, I offer ghee into the fire, so it's from Devdutt to Indra. Like a courier service, Agni carries the offering to that god. So Agni is extremely important.

And Vayu?

Vayu is associated with Marut, storms and prana, life or breath. Vayu is air and prana is breath. They are both co-related. In many ways, Vayu is the source of life. With air comes life and to sustain life you need fire and water.

We see Shiva in the Puranas. How is he seen in the Vedas?

The concept of Shiva exists in the Vedas, but not like we know him now. In the Vedas, he is seen with awe, fear. He is a powerful god called Rudra. Indra and the other gods we spoke of are in the spotlight but Rudra is in the shadows. People are afraid of him. He is invoked last in a yagna, after it's over. Don't invoke in the beginning, he may cause trouble, so there's a forbidding energy. This is not the Bholenath, Shankara kind of image that is found in the Puranas.

What about Vishnu?

Vishnu is more popular. He is associated with the sun, and is one of the Adityas, the sons of Aditi. Here he has characteristics that we can identify with. For instance, as Vamana he took three steps, so he is clearly associated with three steps. You'll find a description of the Varaha avatar as Emusha, and the Kurma avatar as Akupar. There are these glimpses or vignettes which find fuller form in the Puranas. But he is there, in small descriptions—like a trailer version!

What about Brahma?

Brahma is an important god. In the Vedas, he finds mention as Prajapati, Vastospati, Brahmanaspati, but he is not described as an old man sitting on a lotus flower as he is in the Puranas.

His physical form, appearance are not clear in the Vedas. One theory is that Brahma was one of the most important gods of Vedic times but as we moved to the Puranic times, he was abandoned, because yagna was replaced by murti puja or idol worship. Bhakti became more important than ritual. So Shiva and Vishnu gained in importance. And Brahma, along with yagna, started disappearing.

Are the asuras described in the Vedas?

In the Vedas, asuras are not considered negative. In fact, asura is a title for greatness. So they'll say to Indra, to Varun, 'Aap asura ho.' The word which came to mean 'enemy' in Puranic times was actually a title of greatness in the Vedas. In Persian or Zoroastrian mythology too there are devas and asuras. There, devas are negative, and asuras are positive. In our Puranas, devas are positive and asuras are negative. In the Vedas, both are positive. In Parsi religion, god is Ahura Mazda. The word Ahura comes from asura.

Are Vedic gods worshipped even today or has the practice stopped altogether?

During a havan or yagna puja, Vedic gods are invoked, like Surya. In a navagraha temple, the names of the grahas come from the Vedas. Astrology is Vedic. For Surya puja, sukta (poems) are found in both Vedas and Puranas; he's one god who is consistent between the two epochs. Indra may have diminished in significance, but not Surya, although they were competitive gods in Vedic times. In the Ramayana and Mahabharata too you will see them competing. Surya is worshipped even today, in the morning in yoga (surya namaskar), offered water, etc. Surya is a Vedic god who is still alive.

16

Vrata

On any given day of the week, people seem to be observing a vrata. Do the Vedas mention vrata?

The Vedas do mention vrata but not in the sense that it's practised today. There, a vrata is simply an observance before a yagna—like bathing, fasting before a puja, and so on. These observances are called vrata, and the word comes from there.

Why is a vrata observed?

It's associated with karma. Our 3000-year-old philosophy believes that there is a cause for whatever happens in life. There is a seed for every fruit. But you have no control over the fruit whose seed your action has sown. As Krishna says, don't worry about the fruit. We also know that we can work hard but there's no guarantee that it'll produce results. Life is uncertain. When things are not going right, what can you do? You'll be told to work hard, be motivated, have faith, go to a guru or a temple, but that doesn't seem enough. You have to do something. That's where vrata comes in. You undertake a series of activities by which you try to communicate what you want in life. It's almost as if you're communicating with the cosmos, sending a message that this is your wish. By observing a vrata, you express your wish.

How is a vrata observed?

There are different kinds of vrata. One is a jagaran, in which you keep awake all night. It's a shift from your day-to-day practice. There is maun vrata, in which you abstain from talking. The most popular is fasting, in which you decide to not eat, say, from this sunset to the next. Some people take it a step further and observe a nirjala upvas, that is, they do not even drink water. Then there are those vratas in which you eat only a specific kind of food, like chana or sweet food, or those in which you do not eat certain foods, like sour food. Other vratas can be for going to a temple on foot, or going barefoot, on the knees, or by rolling the body, and so on.

Some of these can be quite rigorous, like keeping silent for ten days, not drinking water for twenty. Although men, women, young and old, all observe vratas, these seem to be more popular with women. Perhaps women did more of this because after marriage they would move from their father's home to a new home to live with an unfamiliar man. It would make them feel lonely, helpless and powerless. They would console themselves by observing a vrata—it would make them think they were conversing with god and the cosmos, that they had a connection with the world. So from the psychological point of view, it was a very important ritual.

When is a vrata observed?

There are no fixed days. Some are observed annually during a festival or on a tithi (appointed time) like Ekadashi or Sashti or Dussehra when one massages with a particular oil. Others over longer periods like the Vasant Navratri when one eats only vegetarian food. Some can be random, as when on a certain day someone simply decides to observe a vrata.

Are there any stories associated with vratas?

Yes, some vratas are associated with stories. India's most popular vrata is the Vat-Savitri vrata. This is the story of Savitri which was told to Draupadi and the Pandavas in the Mahabharata.

Savitri is told that her bridegroom will die within a year of their marriage, but as she is in love, she goes ahead and marries Satyavan anyway, against her father's advice. One year later, when Yama comes for Satyavan, Savitri has a long dialogue with him and manages to get her husband back. What this story tries to establish is that the husband's life is in his wife's hands. He can attain longevity by his wife's actions.

Women keep this vrata once a year for the good health of their husbands. As part of the vrata, you have to listen to or tell the story and walk around a banyan tree (vat-vriksha), tying a thread. Banyan trees all over India have threads tied around their trunk. So, there's a story, a ritual, and an observance. The observance is that women consume only fruit or milk, not cereal or cooked food, etc. This is a popular vrata in Maharashtra, Karnataka, Andhra Pradesh and West Bengal.

Is there a story about the famous Karva Chauth vrata?

Karva means pot and Chauth is the fourth day of the lunar cycle. Although it is now observed throughout the country, this vrata is especially popular in north India—Uttar Pradesh, Rajasthan, Punjab. The associated story is of a princess. On her first Karva Chauth, she has a meal before sunrise, fasts all day, then exchanges her karva with seven other married women. The pot contains symbols of marriage (suhaag). She has to wait until moonrise to eat again, but she feels weak and unsure about continuing the fast. To help her, her brother lights a fire far away on a high mountain. Believing she is looking at the moon, she holds up her dupatta and looks through it and completes her fast. Then she breaks her fast and has dinner. Because of this, her husband's body is covered with pins. She is surprised, but Parvati appears before her and explains to her that it was because she did not observe the vrata properly. The next year she does the vrata properly and her husband is cured. There are variations to this story, but, essentially, all of them convey that when a wife observes the vrata properly, her husband remains fine, otherwise she loses the love of her husband or he falls sick, and so on. The vrata is linked to the life of the husband.

Is there a connection of vrata with the Tantric parampara?

Yes and no. In Tantra, there are various schools of thought, and there is not enough information about it. Mantra is related to mann, the mind; when you chant, you are handling the mann. Tantra is associated with tann, the body. Altering your eating or sleeping habits is what you can do with the body; hence the relation of vrata with Tantra.

Tantra is also associated with loka parampara (folk traditions). Vrata stories are not very sophisticated. They deal with day-to-day lives and are rather simplistic. If you pray to this devi, you'll get good fortune; if you don't, you'll suffer misfortune. Odisha has a famous vrata known as Khumurkudi vrata. It's connected to the story of a girl called Topoi who comes across Mangaladevi while grazing her goats. One day, when her brother's wife loses a goat in the forest, Topoi offers broken rice and prays to the goddess; she finds the goat. Her mean sisters-in-law reduce Topoi's share of broken rice when they find out. Topoi goes hungry and offers her entire share of rice to the goddess. Soon after, her sisters-in-law get injured in a bullock cart accident. Topoi prays to Mangaladevi for their recovery, and the sisters-in-law eventually see sense.

This is one version of the story. Another one has the brothers finding out about the mistreatment. They ask their sister to dress up as Mangaladevi and make their wives speak the truth in front of her. They tell Topoi to cut off their noses if the sisters-in-law lie. Basically, all these are folk tales. The crux is that if you pray to Mangaladevi, all will be well, your problems will be solved; if you don't, your life will have problems.

Is a vrata observed for Satyanarayana puja?

In this case, the words vrata and puja are often used interchangeably, while generally a vrata may or may not include a puja. Satyanarayana is associated with Vishnu, and if you do puja, chant his name, burn a lamp, have prasad, sing his praises and bhajan, Satyanarayana will bring you prosperity and happiness. Vrata stories are never about the characteristics or qualities of gods and goddesses but about devotees. There'll be a king, a Brahmin, a woodcutter, a merchant, a man, a woman, upper caste, lower caste, and so on. In vrata stories, the gramadevata (village deity) treats everyone equally, without caste discrimination. There is also no high philosophy here; just a simple ritual of prayer (dhyan), lighting lamps, having prasad, thinking about their stories, of their bhaktas (devotees), etc. Telling their stories (vrata katha) to others is also part of the vrata/puja.

Can you tell us the story of the Santoshi Ma vrata?

Santoshi Ma is the ishta-devi (primary deity) or kuldevi (clan or local deity) of some people in Gujarat and Rajasthan. After a Hindi film was made on her in 1975, this story reached every household in the country. This was the first time that a vrata story was shown on celluloid. The vrata is very simple. Lord Ganesha has two sons—Shubh (auspiciousness) and Laabh (profit)—and one daughter, Santoshi (satisfaction). It's like an emotion that has been given the form of a devi, portrayed wearing a red sari, with a sword in one hand, and granting blessings with another.

The vrata for her is observed on Fridays, when no sour food is consumed, and only chana and gur should be eaten. This is the unsophisticated food of simple people. The devotee should light a lamp and listen to the devi's story, and feed seven children. Multiples of eight—8, 16, 32, 64—are considered sacred numbers, so the vrata is observed for sixteen Fridays. The solah shringara, the sixteen forms of adornment, that women follow are also associated with the goddess.

Santoshi Ma reminds Odia people of Mangaladevi (mangal means auspicious). So a kuldevi became a devi for the entire country. The story is similar to Topoi's story where she is tortured by her sisters-in-law, while her husband is away on business. She has nothing on hand, the only thing she can do is pray and observe a vrata; and this solves her problem. Rather than feel miserable all day, the vrata offers a simple solution, gives you a sense of having done something, having communicated with the cosmos—it calms you down.

17

Storytellers of the Ramayana and the Mahabharata

In all of the Brahmand, who narrated the first story? And to whom?

The first story was told by Shiva to Shakti. It's said that Shiva is all-knowing. However, he was keeping all his knowledge within, staying alone, not talking to anyone, choosing instead to remain in deep meditation with his eyes closed. The gods decided that this could not continue, and the knowledge should be passed on to human beings. So they prayed to the Devi and asked her to marry Shiva and make him share all his knowledge. After their wedding, their conversations became the source of all knowledge. It's known as Shiva–Shakti samvaad, and is the origin of the Vedas and Tantra.

It is said that when Shiva was talking, imparting knowledge to Shakti, all the animals and birds also listened in. They then went and conveyed this knowledge to the rishis. That's why this gyan is called shruti (to hear). It is also believed that bhoot-preta (ghosts and wandering souls) spread certain stories, since Shiva is closely linked with these beings.

When all the stories were written, there were so many that they were titled Katha Sarit Sagara (the ocean of stories). And it all started with Shiva.

Who narrated the Ramayana for the first time?

In the Baalkand (childhood episode) of Valmiki's Ramayana, Rama's sons Luv and Kush narrate it to him themselves. While hearing the story of this great king, Rama asks, 'Whose story are you narrating?' The children say, 'It's your story.' He says the epic poem is so grand, the king is so great that he can't recognize himself in it—'I am not that good,' he says. The implication is that the Rama in their poetry is probably better than the real one. It's a beautiful beginning of the Ramayana.

Is Valmiki's Ramayana considered to be the first Ramayana?

Yes, it is, but whether he put down an existing story in poetry form or created the story or whether he is just one of the many storytellers is not clear. In the Adbhut Ramayana or Aadhyatma Ramayana, it is said that the Ramayana was first told by Shiva to Shakti, which was heard by a crow called Kakbhusandi. Kakbhusandi went and told it to Narada who told it to Valmiki who then composed it as an epic poem called the Ramayana. Valmiki then narrated it to Luv and Kush who narrated it to Rama. Seen like this, whom can we consider the origin of the story—Shiva, Kakbhusandi, Narada or Valmiki?

Why did he convert it into poetry?

In ancient times, there existed the oral tradition. Valmiki may be called a 'writer' but he is actually a 'composer'. For ordinary people, poetry was simpler, easier to understand and remember since there's a tune, a rhythm to it. Anustup Chhand is one of the Vedic metres, a verse format, like 'Hare Rama Hare Rama, Rama Rama Hare Hare'. So the mahakavyas (epic poems)—the Ramayana and the Mahabharata—were composed in poetry form to make them easy to remember.

There's an interesting story about Valmiki. After hearing the story of Rama, he was pondering over it in the forest, when a pair of birds (nara and mada, male and female) flew towards him. One of them, the male, was killed by a hunter. His mate started to weep and kept circling the dead bird in grief over their separation (viraha). Valmiki felt so bad that he cursed the hunter, but his words came out in rhyme. This was the first time his language found rhythm. It is said that shoka (sorrow, pain) gave rise to shloka (poetry). Inspired by this, Valmiki decided to compose the Ramayana in poetic form since it is the story of the separation of Rama and Sita, and it has various emotional elements like karuna (compassion), vyatha (agony), viraha. So he imbued it with rhythm, rhyme, different figures of speech, melody.

Did Hanuman also write the Ramayana?

Valmiki composed the Ramayana in the oral tradition. But in loka kathas it's said that Hanuman *wrote* the Ramayana. In calendar art, he is shown writing Rama's name repeatedly on the stones used to make the bridge to Lanka. We don't realize the significance of this, but up to the Mauryan period, 2300 years ago, nobody wrote in India. We still followed the oral tradition. The first script—Brahmi—came into being in the Maurya period. After this probably the likhit parampara, the written tradition, began.

In the story, when Valmiki hears about Hanuman's Ramayana, he visits him and asks to see it. Hanuman shows him the banana leaf on which he has written it. After reading it, Valmiki bursts into tears. Hanuman wants to know if it's that bad! Valmiki says that, on the contrary, it is so good that nobody will care for his Ramayana after reading Hanuman's version. On hearing this, Hanuman tears up the banana leaf, chews it and swallows it. When Valmiki asks him why he did that, Hanuman says that his reason for writing the Ramayana was different from the rishi's. While Valmiki composed the Ramayana so that people would remember him, for his own fame and fortune, Hanuman wrote it to remember Rama, to discover Rama. This is a loka katha describing Hanuman's complete devotion.

This concept can be applied to everything. What is the reason for doing any work? Is it for one's own name and fame, like Valmiki, or to discover god, Rama, in the work itself, like Hanuman? It is a story of bhakti, dedication and devotion.

Turning to the Mahabharata, was it narrated by Vyasa and written by Ganesha?

This is a popular story. When Vyasa conceived the story, he realized he needed a writer to write such a vast, complicated narrative with so many verses. He prayed to the gods and they sent Ganesha to write it for him. Ganesha agreed, but on the condition that Vyasa would narrate the story non-stop. Otherwise, Ganesha would leave. Vyasa agreed but put a condition of his own, that Ganesha would write only when he understood a verse. And so, Vyasa would intersperse his narrative with such complicated verses that made even Ganesha pause and think. That would give Vyas some time to breathe! It became a sort of competition between them.

Who first narrated the Mahabharata?

In the Mahabharata, it's said that the story is being told to rishis in a forest called Naimisha Van by a sutradhar known as sauti (simply, the storyteller). Those who listen are called shaunak. The sauti is Ugrasrava (one with a booming voice) who had heard the story from his father, Romaharshana. Romaharshana got his name from the fact that he told stories in such a moving way that his listeners got goose pimples (rongte khade hona). He in turn had heard it at a yagna held by Janmajeya. The yagna was called Sarpasatra, where one of Vyasa's students, Vaisampayan, narrated the story of the Mahabharata.

The story goes that Janmajeya is trying to find Takshak, the snake who killed his father, King Parikshit. He is told that Indra is shielding him. Janmajeya decides to hold the Sarpasatra yagna, which will destroy all the snakes in the Brahmand. Rishi Astika comes to visit him and asks him to stop the yagna, because it's immoral. He then tells Janmajeya that a week before his death, Parikshit had broken the tap (deep meditation) of a rishi by garlanding him with a dead snake. The rishi cursed Parikshit, saying he would die of snakebite.

When Janmajeya's grandfather, Arjuna, had burnt down a forest to establish Indraprastha, many snakes' homes had been destroyed. So, Takshak had sworn revenge and bitten

Parikshit. The rishi warns Janmajeya that the cycle of revenge and counter-revenge is unending. His ancestors, the Pandavas, fought the Kauravas not for revenge but for dharma. And yet it was the Kauravas who attained Swarga, and the Pandavas, Naraka. He counsels Janmajeya to hear the story of his forefathers and learn from it.

In this negative atmosphere, where snakes are being burnt to death, Vaisampayan narrates the Mahabharata to Janmajeya to drive home the truth that hinsa (violence) does not solve any problem. So, Vaisampayan tells Janmajeya the story that Romaharshana hears and tells Ugrasrava who tells the rishis, and then we hear it.

So we are the shaunaks?

Yes.

How was Vyasa a participant in the Mahabharata?

In both the Ramayana and the Mahabharata, the narrators participate in the story. In the Ramayana, Sita stays at Valmiki's ashram after being abandoned by Rama, during her second exile. In the Mahabharata, Vyasa has intercourse (niyoga) with Vichitravirya's widows, Ambika and Ambalika, who give birth to Dhritarashtra and Pandu, respectively. The Kauravas and the Pandavas are thus Vyasa's descendants, and he is watching his own grandchildren fight and destroy the dynasty over land and property. Perhaps he composed the Mahabharata to show that violence does not solve problems. He narrates the stories to his disciples Vaisampayan, Jaimini, and his son Shukamuni.

Jaimini's story comes from the Markandeya Purana. Jaimini had some doubts about the story so he went looking for Vyasa who had taken sanyas by then. So he went to Rishi Markandeya who was considered chiranjeevi (immortal). But he had taken a vow of silence (maun vrata). There were four birds who had witnessed the Mahabharata, and Jaimini was directed to clarify his doubts from them.

The story of the birds is quite fascinating. During the war at Kurukshetra, one of the arrows hits a pregnant bird who was flying overhead. The bird drops dead but its eggs are saved by an elephant's bell that falls over them like a protective covering. The birds thus hear and witness the entire war, and they know the reasons for it, the inner thoughts of all those involved.

Jaimini is famous for writing the Jaimini Ashwamedha Parva, which is about Yudhishtira's Ashwamedha yagna that takes place after the war. The parva is a long poem in itself.

Did Shiva hear all these stories of the Ramayana and the Mahabharata from Brahma?

Interesting question. These stories are told in the time–space continuum of the yugas. The Ramayana is set in the Treta Yuga and the Mahabharata in the Dvapara Yuga. Shiva is beyond, outside this continuum. He is timeless or outside time (akaal). He watches the world at all times. Because our time is cyclical, the Ramayana does not happen just once. It's an eternal (anant) story, which happens again and again. In one story, when Hanuman goes to Naga-loka (the land of serpents), the king of snakes, Vasuki, asks him, 'Which Rama has died?' Hanuman is taken aback. Vasuki then tells him that a Rama is born and dies in every yuga, after which a Hanuman comes to Naga-loka, just as he has now.

So Shiva has heard the Ramayana many many times. There was a Ramayana, is a Ramayana, and the Ramayana will continue to happen, over and over again. Similarly, the Mahabharata. This is what is itihaas (history).

18

Lakshmi and Saraswati

Have Lakshmi and Saraswati been mentioned in Vedic times?

Yes, but these words have several meanings. The Vedas have a poem called Sri Sukta. Sri is Lakshmi's first name as in sriman or srimati. In the Sri Sukta, the yajman (patron of the yagna) prays for the goddess to come into his life with cows, horses, wealth, grain, etc.

Saraswati is associated with rivers in the Vedas. There are two schools of belief: some believe that there was a real river, and others, that it is a metaphor for gyan (river of knowledge). The word for her is Vagadevi, where 'vak' means language. If you go deeper into Vedic samhita, you see that language is given a lot of importance. Today, we associate Saraswati with knowledge, but in the Vedas, she was mainly associated with language.

What is their story in the Puranas?

In the Puranas, they acquired roop, physical form. In the Vedas, they were mentioned in the mantras, and you had to imagine what they might be like. The Puranas had a visual culture of darshan (seeing), which followed the Vedic culture of shruti (aural). In that, statues and pictures are made; they appear as characters in stories, are described. You learn about the Brahmand and prakriti (nature) from their behaviour. Other characters, such as Brahma, Vishnu, Shiva, Durga, Indra, asuras, rakshasas and yakshas appear in the stories. A new ecosystem is created and we acquire knowledge from their relationships and interactions.

How was Lakshmi born?

There are two ways of looking at this: one, from the philosophical or evolutionary angle, and the other through stories. In the beginning, there was no prana (life) in prakriti, no living creature, only the pancha mahabhut (five elements—earth, fire, water, ether, wind). Lakshmi appeared along with the first organism because every living being is hungry and looks for food. Food is 'laksh'; from laksh came Lakshmi.

From the need for food arose the need for power—to enable the acquisition of food and to protect oneself from becoming food for another being. For instance, a deer needs power to protect itself from the tiger, and a tiger needs it to hunt for food.

What human beings seek is meaning; we try to understand the nature of the world, who created it, and so on. We seek knowledge, and due to this Saraswati is born.

Thus, Lakshmi is born with the first living organism, and Saraswati, with the first human. This is the philosophical, evolutionary route of understanding this.

According to the stories, Lakshmi is born during the Amrita manthan. When the gods and asuras churn the Kshir Sagar and wealth and grain emerge, Lakshmi emerges too. She is called Varunaputri, daughter of Varuna, the sea god. She is also called Paulomi, daughter of Pulom, an asura king—so she is also an asuraputri. Asuras live in Patala (under the earth) and mineral and grain come from there—this makes her a Patala nivasini, a resident of Patala. So, she is a daughter of the asuras, who is pulled out by the gods and becomes the wife of the gods. These kinds of metaphors and allegories are used to explain a concept.

The story of the origin of Saraswati is a bit vague. One story mentions that she emerges from Brahma's head since knowledge comes from the head. So she is Brahma's daughter, which suggests that knowledge is the child of man. That she has been born from within us, not outside of us. In the Shakta parampara, like in Odisha, Bengal and Assam, Lakshmi and Saraswati stand on either side of Durga; Saraswati is considered Durga's daughter. The idea is that Durga is nature (prakriti), and from nature arise both Lakshmi (wealth) and Saraswati (knowledge). Brahma does not birth Saraswati, or knowledge—he gets it from outside. This is a different concept which suggests that knowledge is outside a human being and he has to look for it.

In pictures, Lakshmi usually wears a red sari while Saraswati, a white one. Why is that?

A red sari is associated with red earth, blood, with life. It refers to the worldly, material life. White, on the other hand, refers to the spiritual world, intellectual, nirguni—formless—world. Tantra gives the colour red a lot of importance, while sanyasis, ascetics, give importance to white.

Lakshmi is the goddess of the material world, so she wears red, and does shringara, wears jewellery, which depicts wealth, power. Saraswati's ornament is knowledge, understanding, wisdom. Real jewellery has no value. She wears a white sari, crystal as jewellery and white flowers. Lakshmi (wealth) can be possessed and exchanged like cash; one chases Lakshmi. You can't hand over Saraswati (knowledge) in the same way; you have to acquire it, learn it. Once you acquire knowledge, it stays with you. And even if you impart it, you don't lose it; in fact it multiplies. If you impart knowledge to someone, your own knowledge improves.

Their personalities are very different. Lakshmi is whimsical, demanding—asthir, or restless. Saraswati is autonomous, aloof, sthir—in repose. Some say that white is the colour of a widow; here, it suggests that she's not interested in men. In the Puranas, by men they mean humanity. So it means that knowledge does not need human beings; human beings need knowledge.

Both these paramparas—Lakshmi and Saraswati—are important in India, one of knowledge and one of subsistence.

A story goes that a child, Ramakrishna (later to be known as Tenaliraman), chants a mantra taught to him by the rajguru of Vijaynagara, and Goddess Kali appears. She asks if he wants a boon from her. While he's thinking, she produces two bowls, one filled with honey and the other with milk, and asks him to choose one. If he picks honey, he'll get Lakshmi; if he chooses milk, he'll get Saraswati. He's torn between choosing wealth over knowledge. Finally, he mixes the two and drinks it all up.

It's said that Lakshmi and Saraswati cannot live together.

This is a concept that emerged during the medieval period, from the tension between baniyas and Brahmins. The children of baniyas, or traders, entered business very young, and didn't get time to study. So, while their wealth was there for everyone to see, they would be deprived of education. Brahmins would study all day—Jyotish-shastra (astrology), Vastu-shastra (geomancy)—do puja, conduct prayers in temples, and so on. They did not have money, so they had to serve and get dakshina (alms). In temples, they would subsist on leftovers of the food offered to the gods as bhog. They felt they had Saraswati, but not Lakshmi; baniyas felt the opposite. This does not mean that if you study you will not get wealth. Today, in fact, if you don't study you won't get a job. It is also not true that just because you are rich you won't be able to understand poetry or can't be educated. In the software world, especially, with the knowledge economy, these two come together. There's another sophisticated idea behind this. Lakshmi satisfies the hunger of the body but cannot bring the meaning, peace and happiness that a human being needs. Only Saraswati can bring that. So Lakshmi provides food, and Saraswati provides happiness.

Sentences like 'where Lakshmi resides, Saraswati doesn't' have various meanings. The most powerful meaning is that when you have knowledge, you will appreciate the true value of money. You will realize that value does not come from money, but from the soul, that money is required only for the material life, for running the household—so your attachment to it will reduce. You will not be obsessed with it. It is said that Saraswati sits by Vishnu's head, and Lakshmi at his feet. He enjoys both—he participates in the material world, but is peaceful because of Saraswati. Indra, on the contrary, does not have Saraswati, so while he enjoys material wealth, he does not find happiness.

Today, for the sake of symmetry, we associate Brahma with Saraswati, Vishnu with Lakshmi and Shiva with Durga.

Brahma is looking for knowledge, chasing after it, so Saraswati sits with him. Vishnu has found meaning but needs wealth to manage society, so has Lakshmi; but he knows her place in his life. When you acquire a lot of knowledge (Saraswati), you value Lakshmi less, because you know you need it only so much; it does not become an obsession. That's why there is always a clash between the two.

We worship Lakshmi during Diwali. When do we worship Saraswati?

Good question. At Dussehra, all three goddesses are worshipped, where one day each is devoted to them. During the puja for Saraswati, students take their books and pens to the goddess. But it is Vasant Panchami that is especially associated with Saraswati. At the onset of spring (Vasant), writers, poets feel inspired. It is said that in earlier times, poets and writers would wear clothes the colour of sarson, mustard flowers (yellow), and compose paeans to Saraswati in her temples. In eastern India, during Vasant Panchami, they also bring an image of Saraswati.

19

Mothers

A mother gives birth to a child. But did god give birth to the mother or did a mother give birth to god?

As interesting as the question is, the answer is not quite as simple. In a temple, the space where a god's image is kept is known as the garbhagriha; the god is residing inside the garbha or womb. Whose womb is this? A temple itself is considered a woman, a mother. Spiritually, prakriti is everyone's mother. Prakriti has given birth to sanskriti (culture). God's mother is also prakriti.

According to the Rig Veda, Daksha gave birth to Aditi and Aditi gave birth to Daksha; that is, the father created the mother and the mother created the father. When you go way back in the past, the division between father and mother collapses. With god, this concept does not hold because god is svayambhu—he has given birth to himself; he is his own mother. Two words are used often in the Puranas—yonija (born of the womb) and svayambhu (who gives birth to self). God is always svayambhu, but his avatars are yonija; they experience birth and death. For instance, Rama is an avatar, so he is born—to his mother, Kaushalya—and dies. Krishna, likewise, has a mother, Devaki. Shiva is svayambhu.

In the Tantra parampara, where goddesses are given a lot of importance, the stories and folk tales speak of how in the beginning of the world there was only a devi, prakriti, called Adimayashakti. She gave birth to three eggs from which were born Brahma, Vishnu and Shiva. She is therefore called Triamba (one who gave birth to three children). This does not happen in Puranic stories. In the Shakta parampara, god does have a mother. In the Vaishnava parampara, god gives birth to himself, and creates the world and its creatures from himself. In the Shaiva parampara, Shiva gives birth to himself; he is svayambhu, doesn't have a mother, but gives birth to all mothers.

Devi is sometimes called kumari (virgin) and sometimes mata (mother). How is that?

In Christianity there is the virgin mother who is Jesus's mother. The word kumari, in India and in the world, does not necessarily mean virgin. It means a woman who is independent, who has no husband, and no man has a right over her. She has no ties and is completely liberated. She is both mata and kumari, that is, an independent mother. Her hair is always depicted untied, to symbolize her freedom. No one can have dominance over prakriti.

In Vaishnodevi and Kal Bhairava temples, Bhairava is her guard. The story is that Bhairava wanted to have a relationship with the goddess; the goddess refused and cut off his head, saying, 'You cannot control me.' In another story, when Brahma's fifth head wanted rights over her, Bhairava cut it off. Such are the violent stories associated with the kumari.

The symbolic meaning could be that a man's ego prevents a devi from becoming a kumari, which is why he is cursed or has his head cut off. These are spiritual, metaphysical topics.

Shiva was svayambhu, but who was his son Kartikeya's mother—Parvati or Ganga?

According to the Shiva Purana, after their marriage, Shiva tells Devi that he has no need for a child. He says, 'I am svayambhu, anadi, anant, without beginning or end; I will never die. So why do I need children?' Devi says, 'But I want children; I want to be a mother.' An interesting conflict arises here. When Shiva is about to offer his seed, all gods and goddesses say that his seed cannot be accommodated in just one womb; it should be placed in many wombs. His seed is supposed to be so hot that no one can touch it. First it is given to Vayu, wind, in the belief that he'll be able to cool it down, but he fails. Vayu gives the seed to Agni, fire, who too cannot hold it. He passes it on to Ganga and her waters start boiling. The reed forests (Sara-van) near the river start burning. From the ash of those reeds, a child emerges. In some versions of the story, six children emerge. As the infants start crying, Kritika nakshatra, a constellation of six stars, descends from the sky as the children's mother and feeds them milk. Finally, Gauri, Shiva's wife, joins the six children together. That child is Kartikeya, also called Shanmukha, or one with six heads.

The question then arises: the father of the child is Shiva, but who is the mother? Vayu, Agni, Ganga, Sharavan, Kritika, Parvati all stake a claim. So, he has many mothers. Shiva's seed has thus gone to many yonis; it shows that the child is so powerful, he cannot be born of just one womb. Kartik means son of Kritika. In the south, he is called Sharavanan, son of

Sharavan. In images, he is sometimes shown along with six or seven matrika, mothers.

What is Ganesha's story? Who is his mother?

In stories, although Shakti wants to become a mother, the gods don't want her to give birth like other women. If a child is born from her yoni, it'll be so powerful that it will defeat even Indra, the king of the gods. So, Shiva–Shakti's children are not born from Parvati's yoni. Kartikeya is born of Shiva's seed, from many yonis. Ganesha is born from the scrapings of Parvati's body. Again, he is ayonija.

The story is that Parvati goes to Shiva, asking him to give her a child. He says he is not interested in having children as he's immortal. She tells him she'll make one herself; she's the goddess, after all. She first collects the scrapings (mull) of her skin, mixed with the already applied chandan and haldi. Then she makes a doll of it and gives it life. In the Vamana Purana, it is said the child's name, Vinayaka, comes from binanayak (without a man); there are other stories about the word's origin too. Shiva does not like the way Parvati has birthed her child, as he cannot recognize her image in it, so he cuts off its head. Parvati starts weeping, and insists he bring back the child to life. So Shiva gives him an elephant head and that's how Ganesha is born. Again, it is ayonija.

In the Mahabharata, we see many ambitious mothers who want their sons to be king.

In the Puranas, the stories have more of a spiritual, intellectual concern, while in the Ramayana and the Mahabharata, the focus is on wealth and property. For this reason, the men go to war, and the women want their sons to grow up and be victorious. This is presented in a fascinating way in the Mahabharata. When Shantanu asks to marry Satyavati, she attaches a condition that her son will inherit Shantanu's kingdom. She claims she is securing her child's future. Is that the real reason or does she want the high position of rajmata (queen mother) for herself?

There is also a competition between Gandhari, Kunti and Madri. When Gandhari is pregnant, she hears that Kunti has given birth to a son (she used her mantra to have Yudhishtira without the nine-month waiting period). Gandhari is so upset that she beats her belly with a stick. The mass that emerges from her belly is cold as iron. When Vyasa creates 100 children from this mass, Gandhari is happy, because now she has more children than Kunti. Kunti uses up the power of her mantra to beget two more children. She then gives the mantra to Madri who uses it once and calls Ashvin Kumar and has the twins, Nakula and Sahadeva. Pandu asks Kunti to let Madri use the mantra once more as she herself has used it thrice, but Kunti refuses. She fears that if Madri were to produce twins again, she'd have more children, and therefore more importance, than her. This rivalry has been subtly depicted in the Mahabharata.

What about the mothers in the Ramayana?

Kaikeyi's story is the most well known. When she had saved Dashratha's life during a deva–asura battle, he had promised her two boons. The day before his eldest son, Rama's, coronation, she throws a tantrum and demands her boons. She asks that her son Bharata be made king instead of the firstborn Rama, and that Rama be sent into vanavas (life in the forest) for fourteen years. Rama's mother, Kaushalya, is pained and asks Kaikeyi why she is being so cruel to a son who has always treated her like his own mother.

An interesting aspect of this story is that when Dashratha marries Kaikeyi, he does not have any children. The astrologer says that Kaikeyi will definitely have a son. At that time, Dashratha promises her that her son will become king. So, in a way, Kaikeyi is only asking for what is rightfully her due. It's like a court case, a settling of an agreement, where the lines are not clear. Whether Kaikeyi is ambitious or merely asking for her right is hard to say.

Krishna is called Devakinandan and Yashodanandan. Who was his mother?

There are some who believe that Krishna is not an avatar (of Vishnu) but an avatari—from whom avatars emerge—himself. But he is born from Devaki's womb, so he is yonija and experiences death, as is described in the Mausala Parva in the Mahabharata. Now, though he is born from Devaki's womb in Mathura, he is raised by Yashoda in Gokul. So he has two mothers—a birth mother and a milk mother.

In folk songs, Krishna is asked who his real mother is—Devaki who has birthed him or Yashoda who has raised him? Krishna replies, 'Do you think my heart is so small that it cannot house more than one mother? I can handle both.' But the question is who has the maternal right over him? Who can answer that—it's a complex world. The story suggests that relationships are not built by blood alone. Another interesting detail is that Devaki is a princess, while Yashoda is a milkmaid. Krishna's claim that both women are his mothers shows that he has a relationship with palace dwellers as well as cowherds, with the city as well as the village. He is large-hearted and this is why Krishna is associated with love.

In the Puranas, is there a story of single mothers?

The Bhagavata Purana has a story of Devahuti whose husband is Rishi Kardam. The rishi tells Devahuti that he doesn't really want to have children, but he has been told by his ancestors that he won't achieve moksha (liberation from the cycle of life and death) until he has children. But he doesn't want any part in raising that child. Devahuti agrees to raise the child alone, and the child grows up to be Kapila Muni who develops the Sankhya philosophy. It is also well known that Sita raises Luv and Kush on her own. Shakuntala too raises her son Bharata by herself in the forest, without the support of her husband.

Is there a story in our Puranas where a father plays the role of a mother?

When apsaras have children, they abandon them. Shakuntala's mother Menaka abandons her in the jungle; she is raised by Rishi Kanva who is like a single father. When Sita goes back to her mother, and disappears inside the earth, she leaves her children behind with Rama who becomes a single father.

20

Women in the Mahabharata

According to you, is the Mahabharata a story about men or women?

It starts as a women's story, then shifts the focus on men, and finally becomes about women again. The story begins with Shantanu and his two wives. His first wife is Ganga, queen of rivers. She marries him on the condition that no matter what she does after their marriage, he will not question her. She then proceeds to drown each of the seven children she gives birth to. When she's about to do the same to the eighth child, he stops her. Because he's broken his promise, she leaves with the child. His second wife, Satyavati, a fisherman's daughter, agrees to marry him on the condition that her son will become king. Both women put forth conditions that he has to accept if the marriage is to take place.

In the next generation, things change. Satyavati has two sons—Chitrangad, who dies in a battle with a gandharva, and Vichitravirya, who is a weakling. Ganga's son Devavrata (Bhishma) is asked to abduct the daughters of Kashi's king—Amba, Ambika and Ambalika—and bring them as brides for Vichitravirya. Where in the previous generation women were attaching conditions to marriage, in the second, they are being abducted; they have no rights. Amba is in love with someone else so she's allowed to leave. When she is not accepted by her lover, she returns only to be rejected again; once something has been given away, she is told, it cannot be taken back. She asks Bhishma to marry her, but he tells her about his vow of celibacy. Amba is ruined; she has nowhere to go and no one to turn to. She suffers.

In the meantime, her sisters' husband Vichitravirya dies before fathering any children. So they become childless widows. Satyavati says since they have married my son, their womb is my son's. Whosoever puts his seed there, the children will be my son's. This was called the niyoga system whereby a woman could bear another man's child but legally, the child would belong to her husband. Satyavati asks her two daughters-in-law to have niyoga with Rishi Vyasa, who was born to her before marriage. On seeing Vyasa, Ambika closes her eyes, and so begets a blind son—Dhritarashtra. Ambalika gets scared, becomes cold, and so she bears a weak son—Pandu. Satyavati is not happy with the quality of the children produced and asks Vyasa to go back to Ambika. Vyasa tells Satyavati that he's a vanavasi (one who lives in a forest), and unkempt; given the previous experience, he'll need to make himself more attractive. Satyavati is unmoved and rushes him. However, Ambika refuses to be treated like an animal, and sends her maid instead. The child produced is Vidur. He is perfectly healthy but as a servant's child, he can never be king. You see that the status of women has come down a notch.

Pandu marries Kunti in a svayamvara. He has been cursed: if he has sexual relations with a woman, he will die.

So Kunti has to take recourse to have children by the gods—Yudhishtira, Bhima, Arjuna. Although biologically they are not Pandu's, by laws of niyoga, they belong to him. Pandu's second wife, Madri, begets Nakula and Sahadeva from the Ashvini Kumars. By this third generation, women's freedom has gone completely. The world of the svayamvara has given way to a very new world.

Gandhari is the princess of Gandhar, what we now know as Kandahar in Afghanistan. She travels all the way to Hastinapur (around Delhi), for her marriage without knowing who she is going to wed. She finds out just before the nuptials that her husband is blind. On her wedding night, Dhritarashtra asks her to always support him and act as his eyes. But before morning arrives, she has tied a blindfold and taken a vow to wear it throughout her life. Dhritarashtra confronts her and tells her that while the world thinks she is an ideal wife who is sharing her husband's grief and handicap, he feels it's her anger towards the fact that her family had not informed her of his blindness and that she had to marry him because her family had been defeated by his.

So it's not clear whether she ties the band out of love or revenge.

It's not clear in the text. When we read it or see dramatizations, we ponder over this. The point is not why, but its effect, the fruit of this action, which is terrible. When her 100 children are growing up, they have a father who cannot see, and a mother who does not *want* to see. Whatever her reason for blindfolding herself, she doesn't remove it despite having children. So what kind of impact would it have had on the children? Did the Kauravas become who they were because of this?

I've heard that Madri commits sati?

It is there in the story. In the Mahabharata, sati is mentioned. Madri was supposed to be very beautiful and there was always tension between her and Kunti. Kunti had chosen Pandu in a svayamvara whereas Madri had been given to him. Kuṇti was sad that while she had chosen her husband, he had bought himself a beautiful wife. She may have not felt beautiful enough, and so on. One day, Pandu got excited seeing Madri's beauty, forgot about his curse and became intimate with her. He died. Madri felt guilty about it and jumped into his pyre, saying she would follow him to Pitra-loka. She left her children behind with Kunti. So, not only did Kunti not get her husband's love but she also had to raise five children on her own.

We've heard many stories of Draupadi. Did the Pandavas have other wives?

They had many wives. The first woman to come into the lives of this generation of Kurus is Hidimbi, a rakshasi (wild forest woman) who marries Bhima, but whom Kunti disowns as she's not of the same clan. Bhima and Hidimbi's son is Ghatotkacha. In some stories, it is said that when the Kauravas poison Bhima and throw him in the sea, he goes to Naga-loka where he marries a snake and has a son, Bilalsen. So Bhima has all these families before Draupadi comes into the picture.

Draupadi is won by Arjuna in an archery contest but when he brings her home, Kunti tells him to share with his brothers whatever he has won. So the status of women falls even further to the point where she's considered an object, a commodity. Draupadi, on her part, lays down a rule that there can be only one woman in the palace. It'll be her kitchen, her home, and no other woman can enter there. She stays with each husband for one year, so the first husband's turn comes again only in the sixth year. What are the other husbands supposed to do in the interim? Again, the men are important. While the many queens of a king have to wait for their husband, these men refuse to wait. They marry other women. Yudhishtira marries a princess from Kashi, Nakula marries a princess from Chedi, and Sahadeva too marries another princess. They all have children with these queens, but never bring them home; they go to visit them. That becomes the custom. Arjuna has several wives. One is Subhadra, Krishna's sister, a Yadava; another is the nagaputri (daughter of the Nagas) Ulupi, and the third is the Manipuri princess Chitrangada.

Rabindranath Tagore had written a poem on Chitrangada . . .

Yes. Chitrangada was a warrior princess. She hears of the handsome prince Arjuna coming to visit and feels that he may not like her as she is somewhat masculine, so she prays to Shiva to make her feminine. Shiva grants her wish and she turns into a gentle, lithe girl. However, when Arjuna sees her, he is not attracted to her. He already has many wives. He wants to see the warrior princess as he's drawn to the idea of that kind of woman. Chitrangada goes back to Shiva and converts to her original self. Now when Arjuna meets her, he falls in love with her and they marry. A child, Babruvan, is born to them and stays back with the mother. Here, the woman is a warrior and retains the right to her child, which is the opposite of the Pandu and niyoga stories.

What's Ulupi's story?

It's quite an interesting story. During a tirth yatra, when Arjuna goes to bathe in a river, Ulupi kidnaps him and asks to marry him. Arjuna turns her down. She tells him that she considers him her husband, so he *has* to accept her as his wife. Basically she has abducted him and is now forcing him to become her husband. This is a very unique situation where the woman has so much power, not unlike Ganga.

Arjuna agrees to be her husband for one night. She begets a child, Iravan. In the Tamil Mahabharata, Iravan plays an important role. He is sacrificed during the war due to which the Pandavas are victorious. Ulupi is furious about her son being killed. She goes to Chitrangada and asks to adopt her son to teach him archery. She makes Babruvan a great warrior. There's a time after the Kurukshetra war when Arjuna goes to Manipur where he battles his son and is slain by him. Chitrangada then asks Ulupi to forgive their husband. Ulupi relents and uses a nagamani to bring Arjuna back to life.

These women play an important role in Arjuna's life. When Arjuna kills Bhishma, Ganga curses him, saying that just as he has killed a man who was like a father to him, so will he suffer at the hands of his son.

What about the Kauravas' wives? We hardly ever get to hear stories about them.

Not much has been said about them in the epic. The traditional loka kathas, folklore, mention one wife of Duryodhana—Bhanumati. The couple loves each other and is faithful to each other—so he is patnivrata and she is pativrata. Usually, in latter-day retellings, he is depicted as being very lecherous, especially due to his part in Draupadi's vastraharan (disrobing), because they want to paint him as a complete villain.

Karna's wife too does not find a mention in the Sanskrit epic. In loka kathas, there is a wife named Vaishali, and there isn't much of a dramatic story there either.

Can you tell us the stories of Gandhari's and Kunti's deaths?

After the war, when Yudhishtira becomes king the elders stay in the palace with them. But slowly the Kaurava elders realize that they are not respected. Bhima makes fun of Dhritarashtra during mealtimes. When he hears him breaking a meat bone, Bhima tells him that's how he broke Dhritarashtra's sons' bones in the war. After repeated insults, Gandhari suggests to her husband that they retire to the forest (vanavas). Kunti also decides to go with them.

A forest fire occurs while they are there. Dhritarashtra wants to run for his life, but Gandhari refuses, and says, 'Let us accept it, accept death.' Both Gandhari and Kunti die in this fire. It's not a completely natural death, it's accidental. You may call it a kind of suicide.

If you look at the entire Mahabharata from the point of view of the women—the stories of Kunti, of Gandhari—it's a bit tragic.

21

Varaha and Narasimha

Vishnu has many avatars; tell us about his Varaha avatar.

Varaha means wild boar, as in the *Asterix* comics! There was a time when Bhu-loka, the world, sank into the ocean. Different reasons are offered for this. Some believe it happened due to ignorance, due to paap (sins) or in the aftermath of pralaya (doomsday). Some say asuras drove it into the ocean, and Vishnu took the form of Varaha and brought it out. Varaha's characteristic is to dig into the earth. So Vishnu, in this form, scoops earth out of the ocean. In images, you'll sometimes see Varaha holding Bhudevi on the tip of his nose or on his shoulder.

What's the story of Narasimha?

Nara is human and simha is lion. So it's a combination of lion and human. The story of this avatar is associated with an asura who cannot be killed by anything that is human or animal. So Vishnu becomes human *and* animal to defeat him; and he's neither human nor animal. While we see sheer physical strength in Varaha, we see intelligence, strategy and cunning in Narasimha.

But why lion?

Lion is associated with kings and royalty in India. A king sits on a singha-asana (lion throne). To defeat a king, Vishnu takes on the form of a lion. In some images and artwork, a tiger is depicted. But most of the time, it's a lion, with sharp teeth and a flowing mane but always a human body.

There are many stories of half-animal, half-humans in the Puranas . . .

In the Simhachalam Temple in Andhra Pradesh, Varaha and Narasimha have been merged. They call it the Varahanarasimha Temple. Both are worshipped as a combined form; they are not separated from each other. There's a story in which the dwarpal (gatekeepers) of Vaikuntha—Jaya and Vijaya—upset some rishis and are cursed to be born as asuras. Vishnu tells Jaya and Vijaya that they cannot escape the curse, but assures them that he will come down to earth and save them. So Jaya as Hiranyaksha does an evil deed by taking the earth down into the ocean, forcing Vishnu to come to the rescue. Hiranyakashipu, Vijaya, too follows the same pattern. He receives a boon that makes him unconquerable by humans and animals. His terrible treatment of his son Prahlada compels Vishnu to take the form of Narasimha and release him.

This is the concept of vipreet bhakti or reverse love. Here, anger too is a form of bhakti. Hiranyaksha and Hiranyakashipu show vipreet bhakti. They are two brothers, joined to Vaikuntha as Jaya and Vijaya. That's perhaps why Varaha and Narasimha are worshipped together in many places.

Doesn't Goddess Lakshmi also make an appearance in both their stories?

The first avatar of Vishnu is the Matsya avatar, a helpless fish, and Lakshmi has no role here. The second is Kurma avatar, which supports the Amrita manthan, in which Lakshmi is born. But here again, the two are not associated. Then the animals start taking on an ugra roop, a violent form, with Varaha and Narasimha. Usually, Vishnu's image is always relaxed, smiling, with mischievous eyes. But in the images of these two, they are very aggressive. A wild boar, as rural folk know only too well, is a very violent creature. If you hunt it, it will attack you. It is said that when Varaha looks at Bhudevi (a form of Lakshmi), his aggression is reduced. Lakshmi calms him down. Varaha is said to frolic in muddy water because he loves Bhudevi, Lakshmi, so much. In images, Varaha looks at Bhudevi lovingly as he carries her out of the ocean. And when he clasps the earth, his embrace is so tight that mountains and valleys are formed. His tusks sink into the earth from which trees are born. So it's a very virile, sexual, intense relationship with Bhudevi. He is called Bhupati or lord of the earth. In the Shiva Purana, it is said that he was so deeply in love with Lakshmi that he forgot to return to Vaikuntha. Finally, Shiva had to attack him in the form of a bull and force him to go to Vaikuntha—as there was other work to be done!

When he kills Hiranyakashipu as Narasimha, he drinks his blood and becomes extremely aggressive and frightening. To calm him, Lakshmi had to arrive. This is from the Shakta parampara. But in the Shaiva parampara it is said that Shiva took the form of Sharaba, a lion with eight legs, and overpowered Narasimha to calm him down.

People say that these two stories are more a result of the rivalry between the Shaiva and Vaishnava maths, to prove one's superiority over the other. A story to counter this one then emerges. When Sharaba too goes out of control, Vishnu takes the form of an eagle with two heads, Gandaberunda. In many places the two-headed eagle is a sign of royalty. You'll see it in the emblem of the Karnataka flag. This eagle is so strong that it can lift even an elephant.

What is Shiva's connection with Varaha?

Once, Shiva takes the form of a jyotirlinga called Lingobhava or a pillar of fire that has neither beginning nor end. Brahma and Vishnu try to find its beginning and end. That's when Vishnu becomes a varaha and goes deep down into the earth looking for the base of this linga. He is unable to find it, so he returns and acknowledges Shiva's greatness.

What is Brahma's connection with Varaha and Narasimha?

Brahma is connected more with Varaha than with Narasimha. The Puranas are 2000 years old, and the Vedas came a long time before them. In the Vedic granth—the Brahman Granth—when the yagna parampara is discussed, yagna has been given the form of Varaha. In the original stories, that is, during the yagna parampara, Varaha is related to Brahma; these stories do not appear later when temples were built. According to one story, Varaha came out of Brahma's nose. In another, Prajapati, an older name for Brahma, takes the form of Varaha, called Emusha, himself. In this form, he brings Bhudevi out of the ocean, places her on a lotus leaf and creates Bhu-loka. There is no mention of Vishnu here. Brahma is associated with Varaha but not Vishnu. In Puranic tales, however, Varaha is Vishnu's form.

In many images, Hanuman is also seen with Varaha and Narasimha. What's his relationship with them?

This is Panchmukhi Hanuman—Hanuman with five heads. His story comes from the Adhbut Ramayana. You must have heard about Patali Hanuman, one who lives in Patala, the netherworld. Once, in a battle with Ravana, Rama is abducted by Mahiravana rakshasa and taken to Patala, to be offered as human sacrifice (nara-bali) to Goddess Kali. To rescue him, Hanuman goes to Patala (hence his name) and takes an ugra, or violent, form—Panchmukhi Hanuman. His four extra heads are those of varaha, lion, horse and garuda. He kills Mahiravana, prays to Kali and saves Rama. In this form, he has all the qualities and powers of these four creatures.

There's a philosophical aspect to this. If you observe, Hanuman is a monkey who usually obeys Rama at all times, without applying his mind. He doesn't take initiative, is not proactive. So, when Rama is kidnapped and he takes initiative, he discovers many of his own qualities. When you take initiative and responsibility, you learn many things about yourself.

Vishnu's many qualities are seen in his avatars. The Matsya avatar is helpless; Kurma depicts stability; Varaha and Narasimha convey aggression (physical and psychological), strength, the power to strategize. Just as in businesses, people try to get around laws, Vishnu as Narasimha finds a way to block the asura. Through the symbol or medium of animals, he is trying to tell us something.

We hear a lot about the Vishnu avatars Rama and Krishna but not so much about Varaha and Narasimha.

From the fifth up to the tenth century, when royal powers began to emerge, Varaha and Narasimha were very popular. Rama and Krishna gained in popularity from the tenth century onwards. The reasons are not clear. There is a possibility that India's military might have reduced gradually. The rajas guna (royal qualities) ceased to be appreciated in India; Varaha and Narasimha seemed too rajasik. We needed satvik (calm, non-aggressive) qualities, hence, Rama and Krishna.

Another reason may be the advent of Islam in India, via the Sultanate and the Mughals. Pigs are haram (forbidden) in Islam. When that became known to the local population, the importance of Varaha reduced. The kings too felt they should not associate with the form of a boar. It also came to be associated with Dalits, whom Hindus have oppressed terribly. It's one of the most negative things about our society. From the tenth century onwards, you see that Varaha lost importance in pujas as well as cuisine, whereas it used to be cooked in royal households before. It gradually became associated with dirt and garbage; Varaha got a negative image and so has a very minor presence now. We now choose to associate with only Rama and Krishna. They, too, are claimed to be vegetarians just to keep people happy, irrespective of what the shastras say or the fact that Rama was royalty.

Who or what is Varahi?

Varahi is a Tantric devi of the Shakta parampara. All the masculine gods have female counterparts in Tantra. Varaha–Varahi, Narasimha–Narasimhi, Vinayaka–Vinayaki, Shiva–Shivani,

Vaishnav–Vaishnavi. Of these, Varahi is one of the more popular goddesses with a number of temples. In Odisha, there is a Varahi temple at Chaurasi. The goddess here is shown holding a fish; a fish is always associated with Tantra, although some speculate whether it's related to Vishnu.

There aren't too many stories about these. One story goes that having failed to kill an asura, the gods pray to the Devi. She takes on the female forms of all the male gods, and this army of goddesses kills the asura. Although Varahi is an aggressive form, as a sow and mother, with its piglets around it, she is also seen as a symbol of mamata (motherly affection).

In the Jagannath Temple at Odisha, next to the image of Varaha there's also an image of Gadadevi? Who is this devi and what is her connection with Varaha?

This is a local legend from the Sthal Purana. There are different types of Puranas, like the Maha Purana, Upa Purana and the Sthal Purana, which is associated with one place alone. There are many stories about the Jagannath Temple that are associated with Puri's Sthal Purana. The temple has a large image of Varaha holding Bhudevi in one hand. In the other hand is Gadadevi. One of Vishnu's weapons is the Sudarshan chakra and the other is the gada, or mace. The first is masculine and is a god; gada is feminine, a goddess. Varaha is associated with Gadadevi. Bhudevi sits on his shoulder or is held near his nose, while Gadadevi is held near his leg.

The rural folk came up with their own interpretation of this image as they were unaware of who Gadadevi is. They said that the woman above was his wife, and the one below, his mother. They turned it into a saas–bahu (mother-in-law vs wife) story, that Varaha loves Bhudevi and has forgotten his mother.

Gadadevi is basically a weapon, used by wrestlers and held by both Hanuman and Vishnu. It is interesting that a weapon has been given a female form.

22

Varna

We use words like caste, varna, jaat. What do they mean?*

In India, we use these words to understand a person's status. Today, if you have more money or power, or a better education, then you have a higher status. In traditional Indian society, one's status came from his jaat. Jaat is a big word, which implies you're a member of a certain community. India has 4000 to 5000 jatis, throughout the country, across all regions. All those who invaded India, like the British, Portuguese, Mughals, Sultans and Central Asians, observed that an individual never existed by himself; he was always associated with a group. These groups followed a rule—roti (food) and beti (daughter). Under this, one community

* The author does not endorse the caste system and the inequalities it creates. This is simply an attempt to understand how it came into being.

would not share their food or marry their daughters with other communities.

For instance, when Ibn Battuta visited India, he thought they were like kabeele or tribal people. Later, the Sultans and Mughals said these were all different kaums (nations). These were different labels, but the word jaat was always used. The Portuguese explorers called it casta, a word that was used for the jatis in Europe. There, it was about pure blood, or mixed blood, whether someone was Jewish or Muslim, belonged to royalty, and so on. They felt the system of jatis was similar to their system of casta. So, the word caste was brought from Europe to India by the Portuguese. The British further confirmed that usage, and so the words jati and caste came to be associated.

Then the British started researching the origins of the caste system. One group was in India, the other was studying in European universities. While translating the Vedas and the Puranas, they found the word varna. This word, they said, probably gave rise to the caste system. And they equated the words jati and varna; though in everyday language the word jati, and not varna, is used. Varna is a Sanskrit word and there are only four varnas as described in the Vedas and the Puranas. But there are thousands of jatis.

Varna was used in the Vedas. Was it also used in the Puranas and Manusmriti?

The Europeans understood varna as rang, or colour. They had issues of race and ethnicity in their countries, and so they said jati was similarly associated with race or colour. They brought their ideas here, but it is not so simple to understand varna. In the Vedas, in the Purusha Sukta, it is said that society is like a purusha (man), whose head is Brahmin, arm is Kshatriya, thigh is Vaishya and foot, Shudra—these are the four varnas. But here, as well as in the Bhagavad Gita, the implication is psychological—it is about one's qualities, or guna. In the world, any society contains four kinds of people—the intellectuals (Brahmins), the physically strong or warriors (Kshatriya), the money-minded (Vaishyas), and the servile or the service-minded (Shudras). But jaat is used in sociological terms, how society is organized.

In Vedic society, the reality was very different from these theoretical four varnas (chatur-varna). Brahmins performed yagnas, Kshatriyas were the ones controlling land (kshetra), and all others were called Vish (others). It was very difficult to classify cowherds, farmers, charioteers and potters. Who was Vaishya, who was Shudra? Mostly, if you were not a Brahmin or a warrior you were a Vish.

The use of the four varnas to classify jati began 2000 years ago in the Manusmriti and other dharma-shastras. There were so many jatis—Kamma, Reddy in Andhra Pradesh, Maratha in Maharashtra, Jat in Haryana, Karana in Odisha—that they were all organized in four boxes, as it were. The Manusmriti joined varna and jati together.

In the shastras, a new custom called shuddhikaran was introduced. Some jatis were described as shuddh (pure) and some as ashuddh (impure). This is a horrific concept. It was not only about identifying the jatis, but was also imposed on daily activities and cultural practices. For instance, in some houses, you cannot enter a temple or eat food without bathing, as you're considered ashuddh. Menstruating women are considered ashuddh and kept apart. A few days after childbirth, people do not enter the new mother's house and bar her entry into the kitchen, as she is believed to be ashuddh;

this is known as the confinement period. Even if you have fever, you are ashuddh.

But, they also termed entire jatis as ashuddh because of some of their practices—this is a most dreadful idea. The origin of this is not very clear. Some say Manu wrote it; others say it started with the Brahmins, who declared they were the purest. That they sat in temples and those whom they didn't allow were ashuddh. Entire sections of people like the leather-industry workers, cleaners, or workers in crematoriums (dom) were marked as ashuddh. These could not drink water from the village well, because they would pollute the water. Some had to wear a pot around their neck so that their spit would not touch the ground. Some had to wipe their footprints behind them. The concept of shuddhikaran was extremely humiliating, and denied even basic humanity and dignity to these people.

The rishis were disturbed by this, because this had nothing to do with Vedanta or self-knowledge (atma-gyan). They attempted to explain this through the gods' examples. They posed the question: Who looks for aukaat, status? Only those who do not have self-knowledge. One who has understood or experienced the param-atma, the enlightened, expanded mind, will not go looking for aukaat. Shiva, who is a svayambhu param-atma himself, is beyond these shallow concepts of high and low. Once, Daksha Prajapati is organizing a yagna. When Shiva arrives, he's turned away by the king who considers him ashuddh because of his association with bhoots and pishachas (ghosts). Shiva is unmoved. But Daksha Prajapati's daughter, Sati, Shiva's wife, is upset by this, and wants Shiva to be allowed in the yagna. Father and daughter quarrel about it. She says her husband is a param-atma, he has self-knowledge, he does not understand the king's concept of high and low.

How do the Ramayana and the Mahabharata explain varna?

These epics were written 2000 years ago in Puranic times, by which time the meaning of varna had changed. The original meaning associated with psychology, disposition, had changed to social pattern, that is, the caste system. So Brahmins were associated with rites and rituals, Kshatriyas were landowners or soldiers, Vaishyas were merchants and Shudras were the service-oriented. There's no clarity about where people like cowherds or farmers would have been placed. They weren't involved in trading, so could they be Vaishyas? Or were they Shudras? There's a lot of debate over these; people aren't sure.

In the Ramayana, Rama is a Kshatriya, a warrior who bears the responsibility for Ayodhya on his shoulders. Ravana is a Brahmin; his father was a Vaishnava. There is no clarity about any other varna. To which caste did the vanaras (monkeys) or the rakshasas (wild forest beings) belong? Were they par-jati (alien caste)—did they fall outside the four varnas? It is not clear. In the epic, a Kshatriya (Rama) kills a Brahmin (Ravana). That is, he commits Brahmahatya, the murder of a Brahmin, which is a paap, sin. We can see the hierarchy at play here. When Shabari, who is supposed to be from a lower caste, gives her half-eaten ber to Rama, the need for shuddhikaran is brought up. Rama's touching Ahalya with his foot suggests that the impure has been purified.

The caste system plays an important role in the Mahabharata as well. Dronacharya is a Brahmin who is so poor that he has to become a soldier to earn money. By doing this, he starts following Kshatriya dharma. This begs the question: have the bounds of caste been transgressed? When a child is adopted, what will be his varna—that of his birth parents or adoptive parents? All these issues come up in the

Mahabharata. The orderly theoretical structure comes under question when confronted with practical situations. What is Krishna's varna? He is born in the Yadava Vansh but has been raised by cowherds. Karna has been raised by Suta parents but he wants to become a soldier, a rathi, not a sarathi—he wants to be a warrior, although his adoptive father is a charioteer. His desire goes against his varna. This question too is raised.

Karna wants to learn from the great sage Parashurama who teaches only Brahmins, not Kshatriyas. When asked by Parashurama whether he's a Kshatriya, Karna replies in the negative. One day, just to avoid disturbing his sleeping guru, Karna bears the pain of a scorpion bite without a murmur. Parashurama discovers Karna's deception, because he knows no Brahmin would have that level of endurance. He curses him, saying that Karna will forget everything he has learnt from him just when he needs it most.

Here, it's almost as if he's talking about a psychological varna; Parashurama is speaking of the qualities of a Kshatriya. Is it the sociological or the psychological varna that Parashurama is referring to here—it is not clear. The question becomes complex here—is Karna cursed because he deceived his guru or because he pretended to possess a Brahmin's qualities? Varna, rules, jati are issues that arise here, and in Karna's story they play a big role.

Does the caste system exist only in Hinduism in India or does it exist in other religions in other countries as well?

First you have to ask whether the caste system is associated with religion or sanskriti (culture). Both are not the same. Caste is also seen in other religions in India. Here, even converts to Christianity and Islam still follow the caste system. It's also seen in Pakistan, Bangladesh and Sri Lanka. So it exists as a culture in the Indian subcontinent. As for the rest of the world, matters of aukaat or status exist everywhere else. But the concept of shuddhikaran is very specific to South Asia. The idea of which jobs are clean or unclean is unique to the subcontinent.

I always say that there's not much difference between caste system and visa. Remove shuddhikaran from this and there are similarities. There's a roti-and-beti system in one; there's a visa system in the other. Before granting a visa, they check whether you have money; poor people usually don't get entry. If not money, they will ask whether you have any useful skills; for instance, if they're looking for a plumber, and you know the job then you'll be allowed to go there, not otherwise. Without the requisite money or skill you are denied entry into a foreign country—this too is a kind of caste system.

23

Sita and Draupadi

It is said that the wars in the Ramayana and the Mahabharata were caused by the two women—Sita and Draupadi. What are your thoughts on this?

This statement could have only been made by a man. In the Puranas and the Vedas, it's said that the cause of everything is karma, action, which is neither male nor female. In our stories, it is usually the male characters that play a more active role, while the female characters play a passive role. Thus kaaran (cause) is women and kriya (action) is by men. It's not exactly correct because anyone can do kriya and there can be any kaaran.

Both Sita and Draupadi had a svayamvara. Did the women in those times actually have the right to choose their own husband?

According to the Puranas, in a svayamvara, a woman can choose her husband. Like Indumati chose Aja, Rama's grandfather, or Savitri selected Satyavan. In the Ramayana and the Mahabharata, however, it is a svayamvara only in name, because the decision, the choice is not made by the women. The women are won as trophies in an archery contest. In Tulsidas' Ramayana, Rama and Sita meet in a garden and fall in love before the svayamvara. But that is a poetic rendition as the original story is not so satisfying. In the Valmiki Ramayana, Rama comes to Mithila, and Vishwamitra asks Janaka to give the young men a chance to lift the bow. Janaka agrees and offers his daughter's hand to whoever is able to do it. Rama lifts the bow, and breaks it too, and so Sita is married to him. It is not really an arranged marriage nor is it a svayamvara. Basically, she's awarded as a prize for winning the competition.

Rama and Sita's story is always told as a love story but Draupadi does not seem to have the same relationship with the Pandavas . . .

No, she doesn't really. Draupadi too has a svayamvara. Here, an archer has to shoot the eye of a moving fish by looking at its reflection in the water below. Her father, King Dhrupad, knows that Arjuna is the greatest archer in Bharatvarsha, and will definitely win the competition, and Draupadi will enter the Kuru Vansh as a bride; Dhrupad intends to eventually destroy the Kurus. However, matters don't go according to plan. The Kauravas burn the lac house they'd given the Pandavas, who are believed to be dead. Although Dhrupad's plan has been thwarted by this event, he holds the svayamvara anyway, since his daughter has to be married. He is unaware that the Pandavas have survived and are hiding in the forest as Brahmins. At the svayamvara, when Karna comes forward, Draupadi and her brother Drishtadyumna both reject him as a Sutaputra (son of a Suta, charioteer), who is therefore not qualified to participate. No Kshatriya present there is able to meet the target. Then Brahmins are invited. Among them is Arjuna in disguise, and he wins the contest.

He takes Draupadi to his mother and says, 'Look what I won in the archery contest.' Without turning around to see, Kunti tells him to share it with his brothers. How are they supposed to share a woman? Who will be the first husband, who the second? Who has a right over her? All these issues come up in the Mahabharata, which Vyasa handles very delicately. Narada arrives and tells the Pandavas a story about two rakshasa brothers. Indra wanted to divide them, because together they were a threat to him. He sent the apsara Tilottama, who told them that she loved them both and did not know whom to choose. The two rakshasa brothers started arguing and, to Indra's satisfaction, ended up killing each other. This was their first argument ever, and it was over a woman. The Pandavas understood the moral behind the story, where Tilottama was a metaphor for Draupadi. So a decision was taken that Draupadi would stay with each husband for a year, then walk through fire, become a kumari (virgin) again, and go to the next Pandava. Arjuna realizes that although she is his wife, he will get access to her only after five years, due to the rotation method.

You feel a little bad because there is logistical planning being done between husband and wife. But the idea here is to know who the father of Draupadi's child is. That can only be ascertained if she stays faithful to one husband for a year.

Tell us about Sita's and Draupadi's births.

They both have unique births; they are ayonija, a word that's used a lot in the Puranas. It means one not born from a yoni, womb; so, we all are yonijas. Janaka, the king of Mithila, is ploughing a field when he finds a pot with a baby girl in it. This girl is Sita. Seet means furrow, the lines that are created on ploughing a field; thence her name.

Draupadi is born from a yagna kund. Her father, Dhrupad, the king of Panchal, is burning in the fire of revenge. He has a disagreement with his friend Drona over a promise he'd made to him when they were children, which was to grant him half his kingdom. Drona later uses his Kaurava and Pandava pupils to subdue and capture Dhrupad, but returns Dhrupad half his kingdom. Once freed, Dhrupad goes to the rishis Yaja and Upayaja and pleads with them for the boon of a son who will destroy Drona. The rishis tell him that what he wants can be a boon or a curse, shuddh or ashuddh (pure or impure). Dhrupad is insistent and the yagna is conducted. Dhrupad gets his son, as well as a daughter. Since she's born from a yagna, Draupadi is also called Yagnaseni.

Both Sita and Draupadi are in a way adopted. They don't have birth mothers, only adoptive mothers, who are the wives of their respective fathers.

Does Draupadi have any childhood stories?

Both she and her brother emerge from the fire as full-grown adults. Dhrupad is so angry that he literally produces his children only for revenge. They aren't born of love; they're born to destroy the Kuru Vansh and Dronacharya. Draupadi is born out of an actual fire and the fire of revenge so she is associated with fire. She is a fiery woman, not particularly nurturing because she has never experienced mamata, vatsalya, or received parental love. She is an object for revenge. The relationship of Dhrupad and Draupadi is very different from that of Sita and Janaka, who share the love of father and daughter.

Sita has several names—Janaki (Janaka's daughter), Maithili (princess of Mithila), but also a personal name, which is Sita. Draupadi does not have a personal name. Draupadi is Dhrupad's daughter, Panchali is princess of Panchal, Yagnaseni, daughter of the yagnasen, the priest who conducted the yagna. It is as though she does not have a personality.

Draupadi has to go through fire every year before going to her next husband. Likewise, Sita has to face an agnipariksha, trial by fire. What is the concept here?

Fire is supposed to cleanse anything that is dirty, impure or negative. Sita does the agnipariksha to prove her purity; that she has nothing to cleanse. Draupadi's firewalking is to cleanse herself of all the karma with her previous husband, and renew and refresh herself before going to the next one. It has a strong biological and sexual connotation.

We know about Sita's sons, Luv and Kush. What about Draupadi's children?

Draupadi has one son from each of her five husbands. The epic doesn't provide the details of these sons. They are only mentioned at the end of the war. When the Pandava camp is sleeping after celebrating their victory, Drona's son, Ashwatthama, comes to kill the Pandavas. He mistakes these five sons of Draupadi for the Pandavas and beheads them. When he presents the heads to Duryodhana, the Kuru prince finds it hard to believe they are the Pandavas. As a test, he picks up what is supposed to be Bhima's head, and is able to crush it easily. He tells Ashwatthama that had it been Bhima he could not have crushed it like this; this must be his son. Duryodhana feels very bad about it. It is quite horrifying too.

If we see the two heroines, Sita is quiet, silent, undemanding, while Draupadi is loud, vengeful and demanding, like her father. Sita's sons eventually become kings, but while Draupadi gets her revenge, she loses her sons. It is Arjuna's other wife, Subhadra, whose son becomes king of Hastinapur. Maybe this is to indicate that one should be patient in life rather than vengeful.

Were Sita and Draupadi good cooks?

In Ayodhya, there is the famous Sita ki rasoi. Sita's kitchen was about the great quality of food. In one loka katha, a crow grabs a roti that Sita has made and takes it to Ravana in Lanka. Ravana is impressed and wants to know who this gifted cook is. So, according to the story, Ravana went looking for her and kidnapped her for her rotis, not to avenge Surpanakha!

In the Mahabharata, it is Draupadi's thali that is famous. It is said that Draupadi always fed anyone who visited her house. A kitchen that always has food is referred to as 'Draupadi ki thali'.

How did the two women die?

People don't like to use the word death for the protagonists of the Ramayana and the Mahabharata; the word we use is 'samadhi'. Sita's story is simple. After being banished to the forest, she raises her two sons as a single mother. When Rama comes, and is taking their sons with him, he asks her to return to Ayodhya with them. She refuses, saying she's done her duty. She prays to her mother, the earth (dharti ma), and asks her to take her back. Can be called death—you've to decide. Some Assamese stories say Sita is under the earth and still loves her children and wants her children to come back. There are other such stories in other loka kathas too.

Draupadi's story is interesting. The Pandavas rule Hastinapur for thirty-six years, after which they renounce the world and start their journey towards heaven. The first to slip and fall is Draupadi. Yudhishtira instructs his brother not to turn back for they have given up everything in life and if any of them dies, they die. In a way, Draupadi dies alone, unlike Sita. When Sita departed, Rama could not live without her, and took jal samadhi, that is, he submerged himself in the river, while none of Draupadi's husbands even looks back at her. Her story is a bit tragic.

Do Sita and Draupadi have temples dedicated especially to them?

There are a few temples, though not very popular. Gramadevis (village goddesses) have temples, and in loka kathas too. Sita has one temple in Mithila, in the southern part of Nepal, where Maithili is spoken and Sita is given a lot of importance. In Nepal, at Janakpur, there's a Janaki temple. In Haryana, there's a Sita Mai temple in Karnal. At Waynad in Kerala, there's a Seetha Devi temple where she's worshipped along with her sons, Luv and Kush. In Sri Lanka, at Nuwara Eliya, there's a Seetha Amman temple.

Draupadi is worshipped as a gramadevi, and her temples are found primarily in Andhra Pradesh, Karnataka, Tamil Nadu. In Arcot district in Tamil Nadu, you find many temples of Draupadi Amma. There, she is considered a roop (form) of Durga and Kali, and plays based on the Mahabharata are performed to please the goddess.

24

Brothers and Sisters

We celebrate festivals like Bhai Duj and Rakshabandhan. Is the brother–sister bond special to our culture?

Yes, it is. When we see mythologies from other parts of the world, we don't see them giving a similar importance to this relationship. In Greek mythology, Apollo and Artemis are twins, but not much detail is provided about their relationship. In our Vedas and Puranas, epics and loka kathas, there's always a brother–sister story. For instance, in weddings, the younger brother of the bride and her mama, mother's brother, both play an important role.

There's a very interesting story in the Vedas about Yama and Yami. Tell us about it.

According to the Vedas, Yama and Yami are the world's first man and woman. As they near the end of their lives, Yami goes to Yama and says they should have a child otherwise there will be no human being left in the world after them.

Yama says they are siblings and it would be against dharma for them to procreate. This is a classic problem of primal twins. Every culture has its conflicts about the relationship between the first man and woman. How should we see Adam and Eve—they could be siblings, mother–son, father–daughter. Similarly, the Yama–Yami relationship in the Vedas is controversial.

After Yama dies, he becomes the first resident of Pitr-loka. As he has not left any son in the land of the living, he can never return to Bhu-loka—that is, be reborn. So he becomes a permanent resident of Pitr-loka and the god of death.

Realizing the tragic situation, Yami starts weeping. It is said that she takes on the form of Yamuna, the river; some say she becomes Yamini, the night, and dons a starry blanket for her brother. Some say that when the sun sets it becomes Yama who goes to Pitr-loka, and Yamini takes his place as the night sky. So, they are destined to remain apart.

Do the Puranas have stories of brothers and sisters?

The Puranas talk of the Surya Vansh and the Chandra Vansh. The former comes from Ikshvaku and the latter from Ila; these two are brother and sister. Although Ila was born male, and known as Sudhyumna, he later turns into a female. Her children form the Chandra Vansh.

In the Mahabharata, who was Draupadi's brother?

She has two brothers. One is her twin, Drishtadyumna, who kills Drona. Draupadi and Drishtadyumna's elder brother is Shikhandi, who is born a woman and later becomes a man. His story is the opposite of Ila's.

Did Draupadi consider Krishna her brother?

In our society, we always wish to give a name to a relationship between a man and a woman. Simply friendship between the two is not acceptable. So this has been turned into a brother–sister relationship; Krishna is Draupadi's rakhi brother. According to one version, when Krishna kills Shishupala with his Sudarshan chakra, his thumb is injured. Draupadi tears the end of her sari and ties it around his bleeding thumb. It is said that this is the origin of the custom of tying rakhi. Krishna tells her that she is now his sister and he will always help her in times of trouble. And because she ties a piece of cloth, he gives her seemingly endless lengths of garment during the vastraharan.

Did the Kauravas and the Pandavas have a sister?

When the Kauravas and the Pandavas are born, it is felt that there should be at least one girl too, because all the queens have given birth only to boys. So, Dushala is born to Gandhari. Dushala's husband is Jayadrath, the king of Sindh, a characterless man. Once, during the Pandavas' exile, he tries to rape Draupadi, but the Pandavas save her in time. They want to kill Jayadrath, but Draupadi asks them to forgive him, otherwise their sister will be widowed.

The Mahabharata also has other siblings—Kripa–Kripi, Hidimba–Hidimbi, Rukmi–Rukmini—it's easy to remember these names! Tell us their stories.

Shantanu finds an infant brother and sister in the forest. He discovers that they are a rishi's children so he brings them home. They are Kripa and Kripi. Kripa grows up to become an accomplished teacher of martial arts and Kripi marries Dronacharya. Drona is poor and needs a job, so Kripa gets him the job of teacher of the Kauravas and the Pandavas. Both Kripa and Drona become their teachers, eventually fighting from the Kauravas' side in Kurukshetra.

When the Pandavas have to hide in the forest after their Lakshagraha, lac palace, is burnt down, they meet the rakshasas Hidimba and Hidimbi. Bhima kills Hidimba in combat. Hidimbi is so awed by Bhima's strength that she falls in love with him and marries him.

Rukmi and Rukmini are the prince and princess of Chedi. Rukmi wants his sister to marry Shishupala, but she is in love with Krishna. When Rukmi tries to stop her wedding to Krishna, Krishna becomes angry and goes to kill him. Rukmini pleads on behalf of her brother so Krishna lets him off but shaves half his head and moustache as a mark of humiliation. Rukmi ends up hating Krishna for the rest of his life. In the Mahabharata, he tries to take the Kauravas' side, but they reject him; as do the Pandavas. So he's one of those few characters who do not participate in the war at all.

There's a Lakshman and Lakshmana too.

These are Duryodhana's children. Lakshman wants to marry Balarama's daughter Vatsala (also called Shashirekha in some stories). But she wants to wed Arjuna's son Abhimanyu. However, Balarama is reluctant to marry his daughter into the Pandava family who are on their way to exile in the forest after losing the game of dice. Abhimanyu feels bad about it and speaks to his cousin Ghatotkacha to help him. After much drama, Vatsala is married to Abhimanyu. These are parallel stories. Balarama had wanted his sister Subhadra to marry Duryodhana but she ended up marrying Arjuna. He wanted his daughter to marry Duryodhana's son, but she marries Arjuna's son.

Lakshmana is Duryodhana's daughter. There's a romance between her and Krishna's son Samba. To elope with her, Samba arrives in Hastinapur, where Duryodhana catches him and puts him in jail. The Yadava army marches on Hastinapur, demanding his release. A huge argument ensues. Balarama is so angry that he says he'll destroy Hastinapur with his weapon (hal). Duryodhana asks for forgiveness because Balarama is his guru and sends his daughter to the Yadava household.

So, there is no brother–sister story about Lakshman-Lakshmana here. Perhaps Vyasa wanted to depict the complex relationships between the Yadavas, Kauravas and Pandavas through their stories.

Krishna marries his sister to Arjuna . . .

Krishna's sister is Subhadra. The Jagannath Temple in Puri is the only temple where Subhadra and her two brothers, one on either side, are placed in the garbhagriha (inner sanctum). Both brothers love their sister immensely. However, Balarama wants her to marry the Kaurava Duryodhana and Krishna wants her to marry the Pandava Arjuna. Everything in the Mahabharata becomes about a battle for territory.

Let's talk about the Ramayana; perhaps that has simpler relationships.

Here, the most important brother–sister relationship is that of Surpanakha and Ravana. According to a story found mainly in the Tamil and Telugu loka kathas, he accidentally kills his sister's husband Vidyutjeev. He then gives her the freedom to pick anyone she wants as her husband; to enjoy any man she wants in the forest.

She meets Rama in the forest and tries to seduce him. When she fails, she propositions Lakshmana instead. This leads to an altercation in which Lakshmana angrily cuts off her nose. When Surpanakha narrates the story to her brother Ravana, she instigates him by saying it was his humiliation, and that the beautiful woman with the arrogant brothers—Sita—should be the pride of Ravana's Lanka.

Does Rama also have a sister?

There are stories of his sister in loka kathas and in the oral tradition, not in the Valmiki Ramayana. In the Mahabharata, a girl called Shanta is mentioned, who is adopted by King Rompad from her father Dashratha. Perhaps, this is Rama's sister. Scholars are not sure whether this is Rama's father Dashratha or someone else by that name.

In loka kathas, one of the popular stories is that Shanta is upset when Rama abandons Sita in the forest. She leads all the women of the palace to protest to Rama about it. When a golden statue of Sita is brought, she considers it as an insult to Sita. Where Rama's mothers and everyone else keeps quiet about this, she becomes the voice of the palace women as Rama's elder sister.

There is never any talk of Shiva's family. Did he not have any brothers or sisters?

Shiva is svayambhu so he has no brothers or sisters. In south Indian temples it is believed that Parvati's brother is Vishnu.

This is a temple tradition, not prevalent in the rest of India. At Shiva Kalyanam, or Shiva's wedding, Vishnu performs the role of Parvati's brother. In the Padma Purana, Kartikeya and Ganesha are said to have a sister—Ashok sundari. It's just a brief description in an oral tradition. In Bengali loka kathas, Shiva is said to have a daughter called Mansa who is worshipped when there's a snakebite. It is believed that she will remove the poison. So in a way, she is Ganesha and Kartik's sister.

In the 1970s, there was a superhit film titled *Jai Santoshi Ma*. In it, Ganesha is shown having two sons, Shubh and Laabh, who want a sister. So Ganesha creates Santoshi Ma as a sister for his sons; she ties them rakhi. There should be a sister who will tie a rakhi and a brother who will visit the sister on Bhai Duj, which is the last day of Diwali. Also, on this day, Yama comes to Lakshmi as her brother. Yama is the god of accountancy and Lakshmi, the goddess of wealth. He comes to his sister's place to see whether she's being treated well or not. And how does he do that? By keeping accounts. Here, an abstract concept has been turned into a story.

25

Characters from the Ramayana in the Mahabharata

The stories of the Ramayana and the Mahabharata are set in different yugas. How come some characters appear in both?

These are Puranic stories where the rules of space and time do not apply. It is a world where people fly, cities fly, people get siddhaprapti (acquire extraordinary powers), they live forever (become chiranjeevi), and so on. You cannot understand this rationally. It's poetry, a way of seeing stories. While we think these happened in two different yugas, in the Vishnu Purana, the Ramayana and the Mahabharata are two chapters of the same story. Vishnu takes the avatar of Rama in the Ramayana—chapter one—and Krishna in the Mahabharata—chapter two. It is not yugas but a story of one kalpa, or aeon. The two are branches of the same tree. They are connected and will always be.

Parashurama appears in both.

He is also a Vishnu avatar who appears before Rama and Krishna in each of the epics. Among Vishnu's avatars—Matsya, Kurma, Varaha, Narasimha, Vamana, Parashurama, Rama and Krishna—the last three are human avatars.

Parashurama has an independent story. He kills Kartavirya Arjuna, a cruel king, with his axe (parashu). His name is Rama, and he is of the Bhargava kul (clan) so he is called Bhargava Rama. Later, because he carries an axe—parashu—he comes to be known as Parashurama.

He appears in the Ramayana. He kills all corrupt, greedy and selfish kings, wreaks havoc all around. All the Kshatriya kings are frightened of him. He learns of Rama of Raghukul who is a very good king and that he has broken the Shiva bow. He goes to meet Rama to see whether he's the one destined to bring back dharma to Kshatriyas. So it is Vishnu as Parashurama talking to Vishnu as Rama. You can't apply logic here; see it as a story. That both of them have Vishnu tatva (quality). As Parashurama, Vishnu kills all corrupt Kshatriyas and as Rama he appears as one to show that Kshatriyas can follow dharma too.

Parashurama is born a Brahmin but turns violent seeing the wrongdoings of the Kshatriya kings. Parashurama has an angry personality and when he meets Rama he tries to provoke an argument with him but fails. He is pleased that he has finally met a good Kshatriya, and realizes that now he has no more work to do. That's his role in the Ramayana.

In the Mahabharata, he returns as a teacher. In Kurukshetra, from the Kauravas' side the maharathis (great warriors) are Bhishma, Dronacharya and Karna. All three have the same guru—Parashurama. It is interesting that three of his students end up on the side he disapproves of. So, Vishnu takes the avatar of Krishna to defeat them all. Through Parashurama the stories of all three human avatars are thus combined in the Vishnu Purana.

We know the importance of Hanuman in the Ramayana, but he appears in the Mahabharata too.

When the Pandavas go to the forest after losing the game of dice, Bhima encounters Hanuman, who is disguised as an old monkey, one day. He asks Hanuman to remove his tail from his path. Hanuman asks him to simply go over it; Bhima refuses and boasts about being a Pandava prince, the son of Vayu, the wind god, and brother of the great Hanuman. Seeing his conceit, Hanuman tells him to move the tail himself. When Bhima is unable to do so, he realizes the monkey is none other than Hanuman himself.

This meeting takes place to break Bhima's conceit. Bhima is a strong prince and says he'll not go around anybody; people will have to move out of his way. This, despite having lost everything in a game of dice. So Hanuman shows him his place.

Were Hanuman and Parashurama both chiranjeevi?

Chiranjeevi are those who live on across ages. This is an interesting concept because in philosophy, everything is impermanent. In the Ramayana, Parashurama kills all corrupt kings, but in the Mahabharata too corrupt kings appear. This suggests that these problems will keep cropping up, you cannot control everything. Hanuman is Sankatmochan, one who removes obstructions and problems from life. No matter how frequently he does this, problems keep arising, age after age. So chiranjeevi is meant conceptually.

Jambuvan also appears in both?

Jambuvan is an elderly bear who always supports Hanuman in the Ramayana, and accompanies the vanara sena (army of monkeys) to Lanka. For some reason he wants to wrestle with Rama. Maybe he wanted to hug Rama; what we know as the bear hug! Rama is a prince and always maintains his distance. He guesses that the bear wants to wrestle with him. He tells him that they'll wrestle when he appears as Krishna in his next birth. For this Jambuvan appears in the Mahabharata as well.

There's a mani, a jewel, called Syamantak that is stolen from Mathura and everyone says Krishna must have stolen it. Krishna goes looking for it and reaches a cave where there's a bear—Jambuvan. He tells Krishna that he'll have to wrestle with him if he wants the jewel. Krishna defeats him in the bout. Jambuvan is so impressed that he offers his daughter's (Jambavati's) hand in marriage to Krishna. She takes on a human female form to come to his house.

Are there rishis too who appear in both epics?

There is Rishi Durvasa who appears everywhere and is famous for his curses. But in the Mahabharata, he gives Kunti a boon by which she can call any god and beget a child by him. In the Ramayana he appears twice. He is Rishi Atri and his wife Anusuya's son. When Rama and Sita are going to the jungle, he predicts that they will separate. In the Uttara Ramayana, there's a very interesting story. Rama tells Lakshmana that he wants solitude. Lakshmana stands guard at the door and promises to behead any intruder. Rishi Durvasa comes to meet Rama. When Lakshmana bars the way, Durvasa insists. He says if he isn't allowed to meet Rama right then, he'll curse Ayodhya. This puts Lakshmana in a moral dilemma (dharma sankat) and he decides Ayodhya is more important. So he opens the door and tells Rama that Rishi Durvasa has come to visit him. Rama asks to meet him but when Lakshmana turns around, Durvasa isn't there. When Lakshmana tells Rama he decided to open the door for the sake of Ayodhya, Rama approves and says, you should always be in the service of Ayodhya, not me. Then Rama says, but now you'll have to behead yourself according to your promise. Lakshmana is shocked. Rama tells him that as descendants of Raghukul, they must keep their word. It is said that Lakshmana then takes samadhi; this is the story of his death. Rama imparts two pieces of wisdom here. That you should always serve Ayodhya (your land) and not give your word so casually.

Any others gods and goddesses that appear in both?

There are many and they are spread everywhere. They are not connected with any one yuga. The Vedic gods—Indra, Surya, Vayu—are seen in both the Ramayana and the Mahabharata. In the Ramayana, Hanuman is Vayuputra, Sugriva is Suryaputra, Vali is Indraputra. In the Mahabharata, it is Bhima, Karna and Arjuna, respectively, who are the sons of Vayu, Surya and Indra.

Were there any rakshasas common to both?

There is Vibhishana, who is also called chiranjeevi. In the Ramayana, Vibhishana becomes the king of Lanka, and marries Mandodari. In the Mahabharata, he comes for the coronation ceremony (rajasuya yagna) of Yudhishtira where he says that he'll touch Krishna's feet but not Yudhishtira's because he is a mere human. He used to touch Rama's feet earlier, who was Vishnu's avatar. To expose Vibhishana's conceit Krishna touches Yudhishtira's feet, referring to him as his elder brother. It is as though Krishna is challenging Vibhishana for making this an ego issue. Then, Vibhishana also bows to Yudhishtira.

How does Shiva appear in both?

The Ramayana is said to have come first from Shiva's mouth. The Adi Ramayana (the first Ramayana) was narrated by Shiva to Shakti, which was heard by the crow Kakbhusandi, and then it spread from there. Rama worships Shiva, and he is said to have established the Rameshwar Temple in Tamil Nadu. Ravana too is a Shiva bhakta. Ravana is said to have composed the Rudra stotra (a song in praise of Shiva) and built a veena called the Rudra veena. Playing the Rudra veena and singing the Rudra stotra, he asks Shiva for a boon—he wants Shiva to go with him to Lanka. Shiva agrees, on the condition that Ravana carry the Kailasa Parvat there. Ravana lifts the parvat, but becomes conceited about his power, so Shiva presses the mountain down with his toe and traps Ravana. Here too he crushes arrogance.

In the Mahabharata, he appears as Kirat to meet Arjuna. A wild boar attacks Arjuna in the forest and he shoots it down. There are two arrows stuck in the boar, one of which could well be a tribal's (Kirat's). Arjuna insists he has caught it. Kirat says it could be his, but Arjuna doesn't care. He insists that he is a prince. At that Kirat says, 'You may be a prince in the palace, not here in the jungle where you're merely a hunter.'

He challenges Arjuna to a duel. In Kirat's roop, Shiva defeats Arjuna who feels humiliated. This is similar to Hanuman meeting Bhima to teach him humility.

Shiva is also a part of Amba's story. Amba wants to marry the king of Shalva but is abducted by Bhishma as a bride for his brother Vichitravirya. When Amba tells Bhishma about Shalva, he lets her go. But Shalva refuses to accept her because now she is impure (jhootha). She goes back to Vichitravirya who says he cannot take back something he's given away. She is caught in this macho, patriarchal culture, and her life is ruined. So she goes to Shiva. He gives her a boon saying that in her next life, she will become the cause of Bhishma's death.

Are Sita and Draupadi two forms of the same goddess?

Both the Ramayana and the Mahabharata are associated with the Vaishnava, Shaiva and Shakta paramparas. So, Sita and Draupadi are considered Shakti's roop. The Valmiki Ramayana was composed 2000 years ago. The Adhyatma and Adbhut Ramayanas were written 500 years ago. Here Sita is seen as a roop of Shakti. A story goes that a thousand-headed asura attacks Ayodhya and Sita defeats him, almost like the Goddess Kali. In this version, it is as though she allows Rama to defeat Ravana—she is Shakti and so strong, she could have defeated him herself.

Draupadi is also considered a roop of Shakti, particularly in south India. In the Tamil Mahabharata, she takes Devi's roop and roams around in the forest at night. The Pandavas see her at night as Devi and get scared. She says she can defeat the Kauravas on her own, drink their blood, but she'll allow her husbands to do it, to prove their Kshatriya-ness. As they didn't save her during the vastraharan, now is their chance to take revenge. Here Draupadi is revered as Shakti amma.

In both epics, Rama and the Pandavas pray to Durga before the war. Usually she is worshipped at the onset of spring, what is known as Vasant Navratra. But the war in the Ramayana happened after monsoons, so Rama has the puja again in Sharad (autumn). So there are two navratris—Vasant and Sharad—both to worship Goddess Durga.

26

Harishchandra

Whenever someone says the truth, we tease them by saying they're behaving like Harishchandra. How did Harishchandra become so famous?

Harishchandra was a king who was known for his integrity, commitment, and for keeping his word. That's one of the greatest qualities of a king—to do what he says—and this comes up repeatedly in his story. He was such a satyavadi that even Indra was scared of him. In Swarga-loka, they wanted to see how far he would go for truth. Vishwamitra decided to test his integrity. Vishwamitra is doing a tap for siddhiprapti in the forest when Harishchandra interrupts him while on a hunt.

What is the meaning of siddhiprapti?

It means to get power. A rishi or tapasvi would do yagna or tap (deep meditation) to acquire special powers. That's how they could give a boon, could curse, fly, walk on water, change form, and so on. You can call it magical or spiritual powers, something by which you can bend the rules of the world, of nature.

So Vishwamitra gets angry when Harishchandra disturbs him, saying he was on the verge of acquiring a great siddha. 'Do you realize I can destroy you, your family, your kingdom?' Vishwamitra demands in fury.

Harishchandra pleads for forgiveness and says he'll give him everything he has. Vishwamitra agrees. Harishchandra returns to his palace and continues his life as king; he forgets about this incident. A few days later, Vishwamitra arrives and asks for his due, reminding Harishchandra of his promise. He says, 'You were just a caretaker of this kingdom, now you can leave it to me.' Harishchandra immediately agrees and prepares to leave with his wife and son without their wealth or possessions; they have just the clothes on their back. Vishwamitra stops him and says, 'People will think you've given this kingdom to me as a daan. But this is to release you from your sin, so give me dakshina to show that this is not a daan.'

What is the difference between 'daan' and 'dakshina'?

Daan is to give something without expecting anything in return. This brings positive karma, and is holy work (punya kaam). Dakshina is fees, in return for knowledge or some valuable thing. So Vishwamitra wants to assert that he's not receiving charity—and that he's releasing Harishchandra from his sin for which he is giving him a fee.

Harishchandra does not have anything left to give as dakshina. Vishwamitra says it is Harishchandra's problem, not his. 'Where do I get it from?' wonders Harishchandra. Vishwamitra asks him, 'What is of most value to you?' He says, 'My body.'

So Vishwamitra says, 'Sell your body then.' And Harishchandra does. He does not get much money for it, so he sells his wife, then his son too, and gives all the money to Vishwamitra.

Some stories say that Vishwamitra claims this is still not the complete amount and that he'd have to give him everything he earns as well. But he can't earn because he is a slave now.

There was a concept of slavery in Puranic times?

In the Harishchandra story, there's a clear mention of a market where people are being traded. Otherwise, you don't find too many references to human trade elsewhere in the Puranas. Greek mythology has a story of Hercules; Roman mythology has stories of gladiators which are all about buying and selling slaves. In India, slave trade surely existed but was not as widespread perhaps, and doesn't appear as clearly as it does in the Harishchandra story.

So he is bought by a Chandaal, and a Brahmin buys his wife and son. They are thus separated. The story is significant because it describes the caste system as well, the hierarchy at play. A Brahmin is superior, a Chandaal is an outcaste, who lives outside the town, deals with dead bodies; he's the outsider. So, someone who was once a king becomes slave to a Chandaal and has to live outside the village. There is an element of tragedy here. Harishchandra works as a dom with him; dom refers to the person who cremates dead bodies and manages the crematorium.

So was Harishchandra in Benaras at this time?

The ghat at Benaras called Harishchandra ghat is associated with this story. The doms who work in the cremation ground there claim that they had bought Harishchandra once upon a time. It's a point of prestige for them that King Harishchandra was their slave. In many places, doms were considered rich because they kept the gold that was left behind by Brahmins on the dead bodies.

Although Harishchandra has no social status, he is not treated badly; he's only asked to do his work. His wife, on the other hand, is treated badly, although she resides with an upper caste, a Brahmin. She who was used to the life of a queen now has to cook and clean and do strenuous household work. It is a reflection of how one's lot can change with time. But she handles it with great dignity. Both she and Harishchandra don't complain about the hard times that have befallen them. This is the important thing about Harishchandra. He accepts his karma, his fate, with dignity. We feel bad about their misfortune just as we feel good about a rags-to-riches story.

Then the situation worsens towards the end. To test him further, Vishwamitra sends a poisonous snake to bite his son, Rohit, who dies in the garden. His mother, the queen Taramati (Chandravati in some stories), brings the dead child to the crematorium. She and Harishchandra recognize each other, but don't acknowledge it because now they're no longer related; they belong to someone as slaves. He agrees to cremate the body and asks for his fees. She says she does not have anything. He insists because that's the rule, that's what his master demands; she can beg and plead all she wants but he needs the fees. So she gives the clothes off her body. The scene is that a one-time queen is taking off her clothes to pay her husband, a one-time king, for their son's cremation. At that time, the gods come down to earth, thoroughly impressed. Harishchandra does not even stop his wife from taking off her clothes, the ultimate humiliation. It's the acme of integrity, the highest level of commitment. At this point Vishwamitra arrives and tells them it was a test, to see when he and his wife would break, but they never did. 'You are worthy of becoming Indra, the greatest king; you are welcome into Indra's assembly.' Harishchandra was such a great king. He kept his word even at the cost of his dignity.

Another story goes that King Harishchandra's life has been saved by the god Varuna, in return for which Harishchandra agrees to sacrifice his son. When Varuna comes to claim the life, Queen Taramati is upset and tells the king that he did not consult her before making the promise, so he should now sacrifice them both. An adviser tells the king to adopt a child and offer that child as sacrifice instead of his own son. A farmer named Ajigarta comes forward and offers his second son, Sunashep, for sacrifice. He says that his wife is very fond of their youngest, and the eldest helps him in the farm. He asks for 100 cows as payment. The king agrees. However, on the day of sacrifice, nobody agrees to do the job of killing the child. Even the executioner says it will amount to paap, or sin, for the child is innocent. Finally, the farmer himself agrees to kill his son, in exchange for 100 more cows. The king is disgusted with the farmer. 'Aren't you ashamed?' he asks. The farmer says, 'No, because now he's your son.'

In this story, Harishchandra seems manipulative, making technical adjustments to save his son's life. It's a tragic story when a father agrees to sell his son, then to kill him for material benefit. The story is also about a king's unscrupulous ways to save his own son while sacrificing someone else's. It is far more realistic; this is not an idealistic Harishchandra. Maybe that's why this story is not so famous.

This story tells of how, in times of trouble, we are ready to promise anything. Here, Harishchandra promises to sacrifice his son in exchange for recovery from terrible health. In the other story too, he agrees to give everything to save himself from Vishwamitra's wrath. In good times, you wonder if you can meet that promise. In the earlier story, he does give away everything. In the second one, he tries to find a way around it. Here, a father agrees to kill his son; while in the earlier story, a father sells his son to slavery. In hard times, in poverty, any man may treat his son as commodity, even Harishchandra. And greed can make you do anything; the farmer rationalizes to himself that his son is no longer his own. It is not important whether the story is true or not. Reflecting on these stories gives one an insight into human behaviour.

What was Harishchandra's connection with Rama?

Harishchandra is Rama's ancestor. Both were honest, good kings of the Surya Vansh who always kept their word and had integrity. They never complain when misfortune comes their way; they accept it with dignity and fortitude. In the Gita, it's described as Sthith Pragya, a person who is stable in both positive and negative situations.

Both Harishchandra and Ramchandra have 'chandra' in their names. But they were both Suryavanshis. How did 'chandra' become attached to their names?

One can only speculate about this from some stories; there are no definite answers. In one such story, while Rama is a good king, he nevertheless wrongs Sita by sending her away for no fault of hers. Due to this, the sun enters an eclipse, and so Rama was called Ramchandra. Perhaps the same can apply to Harishchandra as he too sold his wife.

Another story is that, as a child, Rama was very fond of the moon and wanted to possess it. He was shown a reflection in water, and he thought the moon had arrived in his house. He loved the moon so much, hence his name. It might have been the same with Harishchandra!

27

Aarti and Toran

In our country, why do people decorate their doors so much?

A door is significant because it separates the outer world from the home. Is a door the outside of the inside or the inside of the outside? There is more control inside the house. A door marks the entry into personal space. This is where the shubh (holy) and ashubh (unholy) meet; the negative energy outside should not get in and the positive energy inside should not escape. All these are associated with a door.

What's the significance of a toran on the door?

The word toran is ancient and it means gateway. In olden times, every village had a stone toran or gateway, and wooden ones before that. The Sanchi stupa has two vertical and three horizontal bamboo-like structures. Earlier, they used to make doorways with timber. In Vedic times, cowherds would sit on the horizontal bars to supervise (keep count of) the cows that went into the fields to graze, and returned in the evening (godhuli). That's where the idea of toran started. Soon they started making it using stone.

Around Vijaynagara and at Kakatiya in Andhra Pradesh there are very intricate, ancient stone torans. Even now temples make elaborate torans, and they're beautifully designed. The doors of people's houses used to be small and yet had beautiful carved wooden frames. Above these would be flowers, leaves, grains as shubh chinha, signs of auspiciousness. The doors were decorated particularly during important events like harvest.

So the decorated door is called toran, not just the garland that's hung on top?

Yes. In architecture, the intricately carved top of the doorway is toran. But these days, the flowers or other decoration we use is called toran.

What kind of flowers and leaves are used in the toran?

During festivals, flowers and leaves are used. Usually it is mango leaves, and these days the leaves of the ashoka tree are used too. Ashoka means a-shoka, remover of unhappiness. Mango leaves suggest the beginning of summer, which is quite a bad time, except for mangoes, which represent sweetness. We want to bring sweetness into the house. The flowers are usually marigold. These are special because each leaf has a seed, so even if you were to plant a single leaf, it'd grow into a plant. So it represents fertility. Green and yellow or orange indicate shubh things and our desire for them to come into our house; you see these colours in our flag too.

In farming communities, they would also tie grain stalks to the toran. This was mainly during Diwali to indicate that it is the harvest season, and that the crop has been good and Lakshmi has entered the house. In dry areas like Rajasthan and Gujarat, where there weren't too many flowers and leaves, women would make beautiful designs with different materials like beads. These symbolized leaves, flowers, grains, peacock feathers—all symbols of prosperity, happiness. In fact, if a door didn't have toran, people knew that something bad had happened in the house. When there was a death in the house, toran was not put up for thirteen days, until the death rituals were over.

People also use lemon and chilli sometimes. What's the significance?

This is especially popular in Mumbai. Lemon is sour and chilli is fiery. This is for Alakshmi, the sister of Lakshmi. Alakshmi is negative and ashubh, while her sister is positive and shubh. So the belief is to keep Alakshmi happy but outside the house. Her offering—that is, lemon and chilli—is kept at the door itself so that she doesn't enter, while Lakshmi's offering is kept inside.

What's the significance of rangoli?

In ancient Tamil literature, the home was considered a temple, and the pujari (priest) of the house is the woman of the house. Just as she did her own shringara (make-up), she also decorated the house; and just as we bathe, the house too would be 'bathed'. The floor was sprinkled with water to prevent dust rising, smeared with cow dung because it's antiseptic, and then rangoli or kolam was drawn, using rice powder. It would serve as food for ants, and the diagram was considered shubh and was a yantra (an instrument representing divine energy or power). Good diagrams would be radially symmetrical, again for positive energy to enter the house. It's like a magnet that attracts positive energy; Lakshmi would see it and enter the house. The level of complexity of the rangoli represented how much attention the woman of the house had given to it; it showed how particular she was about the house. An elaborate rangoli meant the woman was well and happy, and the house prosperous. If she was in a bad mood, she'd have made something simple; if angry, she wouldn't have bothered making it at all. It was also a sort of indication for wandering bhikshuks (mendicants) whether to approach a house or not.

North India has more coloured rangolis, while the south has only white ones, drawn with dry rice powder or wet rice dough. It's highly skilled work.

You talked about the importance of doors. In Puranic stories, are dwarpals also mentioned?

Jaya and Vijaya are famous dwarpals (gatekeepers) of Vaikuntha. In the Tirupati Temple, there are big idols of Jaya and Vijaya looking exactly like Vishnu, but with teeth. Dwarpals are supposed to be frightening. Just as if you go to meet a king, or, in today's times, an important personality, they will have a security guard or secretary whom you have to cajole and convince. If they're in a bad mood they won't let you in.

In Shakta temples, the dwarpals are langur devata and Bhairava devata. Bhairava devata looks like a child, but has a human head in his hand, and is frightening. It is as though to dissuade people from entering, or to come only with respect.

In Shiva temples, there's Nandi and sometimes one of his followers, Bhringi, as well. Bhringi's body has no flesh—it is made up of bones—so he has three legs to balance himself. At Ujjain, Mahakaleshwara has a mahavan (great forest). At the entrance are two goddesses, Mahalaya and Mahamaya, as guards.

In temples, dwarpals are also offered food (bhog), aarti is done for them. They are valued because they guard the door. When forts were built, there would also be a gatehouse, where the gatekeeper would stay, as his was an important position.

Earlier, an image of Hanuman was kept at doorways, but nowadays, the image of Ganesha is kept. There is a famous story where Parvati asks Ganesha to guard her door while she bathes. When Shiva arrives, Ganesha does not let him enter and, enraged, Shiva cuts off his head, and so on. Later, he was made the god of the doorway. So Ganesha is both Vighna-karta and Vighna-harta—the creator and the remover of obstacles.

In south India, particularly in villages, they also hang a pumpkin at the door. What's the significance?

In many places, they also add eyes, moustache and a tongue. These are also seen in temples. It's called Kirti Mukh, the face of glory. It was believed that kings hung the heads of their enemies on their doors, after winning a war, as if to say, 'Do not enter, this is my kingdom.' Slowly, as people must've found it distasteful, they started putting up pumpkins, basically to keep the negative energies out.

A (stone) head can often be seen on temple doors. With his large eyes he is looking at the devotees to suggest that even though they may be praying, he can see inside them and know if any deceit prevails. He can't speak because he does not have a lower jaw, but he sticks his tongue out, has large pointy teeth and mocks you. This is also suggested through the pumpkins at the door—they are making fun of the negative energies that are trying to come inside. It's basically an image of a guard or gatekeeper.

There's a custom of doing aarti when we are going somewhere or if visitors are at the door. Why is that?

We believe a lot in shuddhi (purity) and ashuddhi (pollution). When you are coming in from outside, you are bringing ashuddhi or negative energy. Even now we leave our footwear at the door and wash our hands, feet and mouth. Basically, you purify yourself (do shuddhikaran) before entering. Outside temples as well, there is a water tap for devotees to wash their feet. Aarti is one ritual of purification. Fire is supposed to destroy negative energies and only let positive energies remain. When you are leaving the house too, aarti is done to send positive energy with you. So a merchant may be going to the bazaar to trade; soldiers may be going to a battle or to hunt. They need positive divine energy with them for support and they shouldn't bring back negative energies of death and destruction (or ghosts or wandering souls) into the house.

There is a story about Bhanumati, Duryodhana's wife, who tries to stop him, and Karna, from going to battle with the Pandavas at Kurukshetra. But Duryodhana and Karna convince her that that's the only way they can assert their superiority and gain their rights. So she does a puja and does their aarti and wishes them success in the battlefield. What else can a wife do? She is unable to stop them, so she gives them positive energy and her good wishes through the aarti ritual.

In temples too there is an aarti done for the gods. Is this the same thing?

Not really, although some believe that they are removing the evil eye for the god as devotees are visiting him every day, that by doing the aarti, they will replenish god's energy, which the devotees take away from him. In many temples, particularly Vaishnava ones, there's also a custom of not showing the god's image much. A system of jhanki is followed in north India where the door opens only for a short while for the devotees to take darshan.

When a bride enters her new home, there's a ritual of her knocking over a kalash (pot) of rice at the door with her foot. What does this signify?

The bride is considered the Lakshmi of the house. The wish is that a Lakshmi brings wealth and prosperity into the house. This is represented with the ritual when she overturns the rice jar *inside* the house; she brings wealth and prosperity with her. The idea is to let good fortune come inside with the daughter-in-law.

And at the time of leaving her maiden home, the doli (palanquin) ceremony, she throws the rice back into the house, to suggest that she is released from the debt she owes her parents. As she is a roop of Lakshmi, she always gives rice (wealth) whether entering or departing.

28

Women in the Ramayana

We've heard detailed stories about some women in the Ramayana but not about all of them. Let's talk about them chapter-wise. To begin with, the Baalkand.

Mothers play an important role in the Baalkand. Dashratha has three wives—Kaushalya, Kaikeyi and Sumitra. Not much is said about these women. Kaushalya hailed from Kosala, which was divided into two parts. One side was ruled by Dashratha, and the other by Kaushalya's brother. To maintain peace, Kaushalya was married off to Dashratha.

There is an interesting story about Kaikeyi. She was from the kingdom of Kaikey, which is now in Pakistan. The horses of this land were famous, hence her father was called Ashwapati—the keeper of horses, where ashwa is horse. He knew the language of animals. However, he had been told that he would die if he shared that knowledge with anyone.

Once, when he is sitting in the garden with his wife (Kaikeyi's mother), he overhears a conversation between two swans (hansa) and laughs. His wife asks him what he heard, and he says he cannot tell her. Unthinkingly, his wife says, 'If you love me, you'll tell me.' The king wonders what kind of a wife does not care about her husband's life. He abandons her. So Kaikeyi grows up without a mother. Manthara raises her.

When Rama was being taught by Vishwamitra, did he meet any women?

Women play an important role during Rama's education by Vasishtha and Vishwamitra. When Rama goes into the forest, he engages with women at different levels. One is violent—he kills a rakshasi called Tadaka. Thus, the very first battle he wins is against a woman. And the other is kindness—the very first person he protects is also a woman, named Ahilya. He kills one woman, and saves another. He is taught that a king has to be ruthless sometimes. When he hesitates to kill a woman, he is told not to look at the gender but at her actions. With Ahilya, he must repair her wrong, which may've been an accident—something which only a king can do. Rama learns about the two extreme aspects of a king—violent and kind.

We haven't heard much about Lakshmana's wife, Urmila.

The four wives of the four brothers were—Sita, Urmila, Shrutakirti and Mandavi, all King Janaka's daughters. Urmila's stories are found in loka kathas. One story is about how Lakshmana is approached by Nidradevi (sleep) when he is in the forest with Rama. He tells Nidradevi that he cannot sleep because he has to serve Rama day and night. Instead, she should go to his wife, Urmila, and ask her to take his exhaustion and his sleep. Urmila accepts. As a result, she sleeps during the day for her husband and at night for herself. Almost like Sleeping Beauty, she sleeps for fourteen years. And Lakshmana never gets tired. In this way, both husband and wife serve Rama and Sita.

When Rama is in the forest, does he meet other women?

Here too women play an important role. It is said that when Sita is preparing to go to the forest, she starts wearing clothes appropriate for the forest—the clothes made of bark that the wives of rishis wore. The women of the palace object. Sita is a kulvadhu, bride of the clan, and cannot dress like a sanyasin, or someone who has renounced worldly life. She should dress like a bride, otherwise there will be a negative influence, a bad omen, and it will bring bad luck into the home. So Sita goes like a princess to the forest although it's depicted otherwise in pictures. In those times, it was believed that the 'ghar ki Lakshmi', the devi of the house, should always be well dressed and made-up, and look happy, otherwise it'd be bad luck for the household.

In the jungle, when Rama, Sita and Lakshmana go to Rishi Atri's ashram, they meet his wife, Anusuya. She too advises Sita about shringara, and gives her a garment which will never get dirty. Through the fourteen years that Sita is in the forest, her clothes are always clean and beautiful.

The other famous encounter Rama has is with Surpanakha. She is a woman of the forest and wants to have relations with Rama, who refuses. Then Lakshmana also turns her down, and cuts off her nose. It's a very violent episode.

There are many loka kathas about Surpanakha as well, especially in the south Indian tradition. One talks of her husband, Vidyutjeev. There's an argument between him and her brother, Ravana, during which Vidyutjeev, who has a big tongue and mouth, gobbles Ravana up. Ravana then asks Surpanakha to pull him out of her husband's stomach. Surpanakha knows that if she does so, she will lose her husband. Ravana promises to make her son the uttaradhikari, the heir to the throne, if she saves him. So Surpanakha pulls her brother out, and her husband dies. Later, Ravana forgets his promise and makes his son, Meghnad, the heir. Surpanakha is roaming around in the forest, distrustful of all men. Here, Lakshmana accidentally kills her son. Surpanakha goes looking for her son's killer and comes upon Rama. Seeing his beauty and grace, she falls in love with him, and forgets all her brother's wrongdoings and the murder of her son. You find many such stories in loka kathas.

This story about Lakshmana cutting off Surpanakha's nose is a very violent one; there's also Tadaka's story.

There are stories in the Ramayana about violence against women. Surpanakha's story is significant. She is sexually aroused, wants to have relations with these handsome men; she is a rakshasi and has no understanding of marriage, fidelity, etc. She is simply following her desires. To stop her, rather than just push her away, they cut off her nose. After this incident, Rama's life is invaded by misfortune and sorrow. Sita is abducted, there's a war; even after they return to Ayodhya, he has to give up Sita. Rama and Sita's relationship breaks down. This incident is a turning point. This is to show karma. You may feel you have done a good deed but every action bears a fruit.

When Sita goes to Lanka, does she meet women there?

Yes, Sita meets many rakshasis in the Ashoka Vatika (garden) where Ravana keeps her. There's Ravana's favourite queen, Mandodari, and Vibhishana's wife (in some stories, daughter) Trijata, with whom Sita becomes good friends. Trijata is the positive influence on her. Other women push her to marry Ravana, wondering why any woman would resist a great ruler like him. There's of course Surpanakha too who keeps pestering her.

What was Sita's relationship with Mandodari like? I've heard she used to help Sita and keep asking Ravana to send her back to Rama.

In Lanka, there were many characters who would tell Ravana that keeping Sita against her will was not right. But Ravana would remain adamant. He would say he was avenging his sister's (Surpanakha's) insult, but actually it was to appease his ego and sexual desire. So there was a lot of tension in his household.

In one of the loka kathas, Sita is Mandodari's daughter. This version has become quite popular now. According to this story, a rishi predicts that Mandodari's daughter will become the reason for Ravana's death—his nemesis. So Mandodari throws her infant daughter into the ocean. This child is given by the ocean to Bhudevi, who lets Janaka find her. This child grows up to become Sita.

Are there any important women Rama meets in Kishkinda?

Yes, this is after Sita's abduction when he wanders the land, looking for her. On the way, he meets Vedavati, who is doing tap because she wants to marry Vishnu. She recognizes Rama as Vishnu's avatar and asks to marry him. He tells her he cannot marry her in this birth, but that in another yuga, in another birth, he will. It is believed that as Vaishnodevi, she waits to marry Vishnu.

There's also Shabari's story—Shabari feeds Rama ber.

When he finally reaches the monkey kingdom (vanara desh), Kishkinda, he finds that Vali has forcibly captured Sugriva's wife, Ruma. Vali's own wife is Tara. These are the two significant women in this part of the tale. When Vali is killed, Tara marries Sugriva and becomes his favourite queen. In some stories, Tara curses Rama, saying that since he killed her husband, he will suffer the loss of his wife—a second time. That he will die of patni-viyog (separation from wife), which does come true later.

In the Sundarkand, when Hanuman goes to Lanka, he meets women. Tell us about them.

In the story of Hanuman's adventures, women are very important. First, he meets a yogini called Swayamprabha in a cave. She gives him food and offers him the bounties of the cave. She asks him to stay back with her instead of going to Lanka in search of someone else's wife. He refuses, saying he is bound by his duty towards Rama. Later, when he has to leap across the ocean to reach Lanka, all the obstacles in his path are in the form of women, like Surasa and Simhika. Simhika is a rakshasi who swallows him completely. Hanuman grows in size inside her stomach and bursts out. This is yet another instance of a woman being killed. In Lanka, he battles Lankini, who is the guardian or gramadevi (village goddess) of the land. Her defeat symbolizes the certain defeat of Lanka itself.

Normally, violence against women would be considered improper, but in the Ramayana, such stories occur repeatedly. One can speculate whether it signifies the killing vasna—lust, desire. After the advent of Buddhism, when vairagi (ascetic) religions started developing, women signified temptation. They would enchant and seduce rishis, who had to resist them. In stories, these got translated into violence against women.

Do they figure in stories of war?

There are no women on the battlefield, but when Meghnad is killed by Lakshmana, Meghnad's head reaches Lanka. His wife, Sulochana, receives his head, while his body remains on the battlefield. The other rakshasas are scared to go back for the body. Sulochana goes to Ravana and declares that she herself will go to the battlefield to get the body. Ravana tries to stop her, saying it would be suicidal. She asks him why he let his son go when he knew it was suicidal. Ravana says it was Meghnad's duty as the prince of Lanka, and it would have been shameful if he had fled the battlefield. Sulochana then goes to Rama and asks for her husband's body to be given to her, as she wants to perform his last rites. Lakshmana says Meghnad had come there to kill them, so he should ideally make an example of Meghnad's body to send a message to Lanka. Sulochana points out that her husband was no different from Rama himself, who too obeyed his father's orders. Rama is convinced and agrees. He asks for her forgiveness and orders that Meghnad's body be respectfully given to Sulochana. Rama says the woman had proved that rakshasas too have dharma and decency (sabhyata). Rama admires her dignity. She is called Sati Sulochana, that is, noble woman.

In Thailand, I heard a story about a golden mermaid in the Ramayana. Who is this creature?

The story of Suvarna Matsya, the golden mermaid, comes from the Ramayana of South East Asia. When the monkeys were building the Rama setu (bridge) for Rama to cross over to Lanka, she, as the princess of the ocean, would break the bridge because she was controlling the waters. Hanuman went to fight her. Suvarna Matsya fell in love with him and agreed to support the war and not break the bridge, which Ravana had been asking her to do. Unlike the Indian narratives, in their version, Hanuman is not a brahmachari, and marries her. They have a child, Makardhwaj. This story is found only in South East Asia.

29

Uttara Ramayana

The Uttarkand is a part of the Ramayana, then why is it called Uttara Ramayana?

In our stories and plays, we always have a happy ending, called sukhant. The Ramayana does not have this, in particular the Uttarkand, which has a tragic ending. For many, the Ramayana ends when Rama is finally crowned king and establishes Ramarajya. They see the Uttara Ramayana as another poem.

We like to see Rama as god, who is always entirely positive and perfect. In the Uttarkand, it seems as though Rama is no longer perfect, and perhaps this is why people did not like it and began to consider this section not part of the Ramayana. Another reason is that Sanskrit scholars are of the opinion that the language of the Uttara Ramayana is different from the rest of the text. It is as though it was composed later and combined with Valmiki's Ramayana.

In the Uttara Ramayana, Rama becomes king and Sita goes to the forest. Does she go on her own or is she asked to leave—what is the story here?

In Valmiki's Ramayana, when Rama asks his spies to find out what people in the city are talking about, he learns that they are discussing Sita's character. They're gossiping about what might have happened in Lanka in the four months that Ravana had imprisoned Sita. Rama doesn't like it. He feels the reputation of Raghukul is becoming tainted. So he tells Lakshmana to take Sita into the forest and leave her there. So it's not vanavas; she is abandoned.

In the Krittivasi Ramayana, a dhobi's wife goes to her mother's house, but on her way back she has to take shelter in a boatman's house for one night as the river is flooded. On her return, her husband refuses to accept her because she has stayed with a strange man. He says, 'I am not Rama to accept a wife who has lived with a strange man for four months.' It is interesting that this person is a dhobi who cleans clothes and removes stains. This is to suggest that the Raghukul has acquired a stain that even Rama cannot cleanse.

In a third version, the women of the palace—the queens, servants, playmates—ask Sita whether she'd seen Ravana. Sita says she did not even look at him. When they persist, she says she only saw his shadow in the water when he abducted her and took her away in his flying chariot (Pushpak Viman) over the sea. They ask her to draw the shadow. When she does, they feel that she's drawing his shadow in his fond memory. There's even a story called 'Ravana Chhaya'. This reaches Rama who starts doubting Sita.

In another version, Surpanakha wants to avenge the death of her brother and the destruction of Lanka; she doesn't want Rama and Sita to have a happy married life. So, she disguises herself and goes and starts gossiping in the streets of the city about Ravana and Sita. Then she asks Sita to draw Ravana's shadow. Sita draws only the outline that she'd seen, which Surpanakha completes later and shows everyone saying, 'Look what Sita does when she's alone.' This gives rise to suspicion in the palace.

In all these versions, at the end, Rama has Lakshmana abandon her in the forest to save Raghukul's reputation.

Sita didn't even know she was being abandoned?

No, she finds out only upon reaching the jungle. She is told not to return, not to tell anyone she is Rama's wife, a kulvadhu of Raghukul. It is said that Rama did not tell her because whenever he had spoken to her about something she, being an intelligent woman, had argued back. Like she had done when Rama had not wanted her to join him in his vanavas; she made him reverse his decision by her sharp logic. We worship Raja Rama (the king), not Pati Rama (the husband). The important point here is that Rama does not remarry.

In the Ramayana, Rama has been shown to cry thrice—once when Sita is abducted by Ravana, the second time when Rama abandons her, and the third time when she goes back into the earth.

People say that because Rama treated his wife badly, even today women are not respected by men in India.

This is known as kutark, or misplaced logic. If our youth, our men, wished to emulate Rama so much, then they would be maryada purushottam like him; they would follow rules and have high morals. How many Indian men do so? There would be no corruption if they indeed followed Rama's example. Rama was ekampatnivrata (monogamist); not all Indian men are. Indian men don't seem to have adopted any qualities of Rama other than the negative.

This epic is not meant to be a parable, a story with a moral. Both the Ramayana and the Mahabharata are mythological tales, mahakavya (great poems), which are simply telling stories, not suggesting you become like the characters. But having heard these stories, you can reflect on what the characters went through, what their dharma sankats (moral dilemmas) were, what decisions they took and how.

Rama is conflicted about his role as a king and husband. Ultimately, he follows the cardinal rule of Raghukul that the king's reputation is above all else; he may even have to sacrifice his personal happiness for it. He will not be respected by his people if he is even slightly tainted. So as king, Rama has to leave Sita, his queen, which means he ends up losing his wife too. If he had remarried, the story would have been different. The Ramayana may not even have been written.

What's the story of Luv and Kush's birth?

When he abandons her, Rama does not know Sita is pregnant. One version of the story goes that Sita goes to Valmiki's ashram and stays there where her two sons—Luv and Kush—are born.

Another version says that only one child—Luv—is born. One day Sita leaves the toddler in Valmiki's care in the ashram and goes to the river to bathe. Valmiki is distracted as he's composing the Ramayana, and the boy vanishes. He goes looking for him and when he can't find him, in a panic, he creates another child from the kusha grass, using a mantra. He names this child, who looks exactly like Luv, Kush. Sita returns, having found the wandering Luv, and sees his lookalike in Valmiki's lap.

They live in the jungle where Sita teaches the children archery. As instructed, she has not told anyone that she is Rama's wife. But she wants her children to hear good things about Rama. So Valmiki teaches them his poem, the Ramayana.

It's said that Valmiki could not decide a title for the poem. His first idea was Ramayana—the story of Rama. Another was Pulatsya Vadham, that is, the destruction of the Pulatsya Vansh, to which Ravana belonged. Another was Sita Charitam (the story of Sita), because she's an important character. Sita suggests that he call it the Ramayana because it is the longest story. She also wants to ensure that people think good things about Rama.

The Uttarkand also has the important story of the Ashwamedha yagna. Tell us about it.

In Vedic times, a king would perform this yagna in which a horse is let loose, and wherever the horse roams unopposed, that becomes the king's territory. Rama also does this yagna.

At that time, many writers, poets, storytellers come to the court to show their work. Luv and Kush too come, and narrate the Ramayana to him. Rama asks them where they'd heard this story, which was his own, and they tell him that Rishi Valmiki had taught them. He says it can't really be his story because the Rama in their story is too great a man, not like him.

He asks them what they would like as a reward. They say they don't want anything other than to meet his queen, Sita. Rama shows them an idol of Sita next to the throne, and tells them she had to leave for the forest because his people saw her as a tainted woman. They are surprised that the great woman for whom such a huge war was fought had been ill-treated like this and does not have a place in his kingdom.

They return to the ashram and tell Sita that Rama is not so great after all; he abandoned his wife. When the Ashwamedha horse reaches the ashram, and they find out it is Rama's, they refuse to accept his rule. They stop the horse. In the ensuing battle between Rama's army and the boys, Rama's army, including his brothers and Hanuman, is defeated. Finally, Rama arrives and picks up his Brahmastra. That's when Sita stops him and tells him that they are his children. After the truth is revealed, the family is briefly reunited.

At this time, Rama says that he had abandoned the queen not the wife. In order to perform the Ashwamedha yagna, a king needs a wife; if he'd indeed abandoned his wife, he'd have had to remarry. But he did not. Instead he installed a gold idol of Sita. Gold is a pure metal. So Rama believed his wife was pure, but the rules of Raghukul dictated that his reputation remain untarnished at all costs. People think this would be a happy ending, and request her to return to the kingdom. Sita says she does not want to live in a kingdom where reputation was more important than love. 'I've raised two good, strong children who have proved their worth by defeating even Rama's army,' she says. 'So let them go with their father, and I will go back to my mother.' At that, the earth, her mother, opens up and takes her in. This is how Sita departs.

Does the Uttarkand end here?

There are many stories in the Uttarkand, but basically, once Sita is gone, Rama rules for a few years more, until his children grow up. He then takes jal samadhi as he cannot live without Sita. He walks into the Sarayu river and never returns.

In the Uttara Ramayana, Rama had beheaded Rishi Shambuka. Is this story caste related?

A story goes that one day a Brahmin comes into the king's court carrying his dead son and says that there is no dharma in Ramarajya, that his son died before him when it should be the other way around. When Rama asks Narada how this could happen, Narada says that every yuga has a different system. In the Kriti Yuga, only Brahmins could become sanyasis, in the Treta Yuga, Kshatriyas too could become sanyasis, in the Dvapara Yuga, even Vaishyas could become sanyasis and in Kali Yuga, anyone can become a sanyasi. Rama is in Dvapara Yuga, and a Shudra—Rishi Shambuka—has become a sanyasi, thus upsetting the system and causing problems. Rama wonders why there would be a problem if a Shudra takes sanyas. Narada explains that there is now imbalance in the system and as king, it is Rama's duty to restore the balance.

Rama goes to Shambuka, who says he's performing tap for moksha prapti (liberation), and wishes to go to Vishnu-loka. He is unwilling to return to ordinary life and follow his jati dharma. Rama is torn. Here is a man striving for moksha and you want to pull him back into the social structure of the caste system. So Rama beheads him and releases him.

This is the negative side of maryada purushottam. There are two sides to this persona. As a follower of rules, in the first part of the Ramayana, Rama is an ideal man and loved by all. In the second half, we see the other side of rules, that there is no freedom. When rules become too rigid, and the order of society is made paramount, many people get crushed, like Sita and Shambuka. This story is for future kings and rulers, to understand the negative aspect of unbending rules.

30

Yayati

Who is Yayati?

Yayati was a Chandravanshi king and his descendants play a big role towards the end of the Mahabharata. His relation is with the characters of the Mahabharata.

There's some interesting story about his wives . . .

Very interesting. He had two wives—Devyani and Sharmishta. But it's a complicated relationship. Devyani is the daughter of Shukracharya, the guru of the asuras. Sharmishta is the daughter of the king of asuras, Vrishparva. One is a princess and the other is a Brahmin's daughter. Both are friends. In Puranic times, the relationship between a rishi and a king was complex. A king sits on the throne, lives in the palace, and takes the advice of a rishi who lives in the forest. In terms of power, the raja is superior, but in terms of knowledge, he is dependent on the rishi. The raja gives the rishi a lot of importance, touches his feet, but the rishi salutes the king because he is the king. The tension in their relationship is depicted through their daughters.

Once, the girls go bathing in the river. After the bath, they wear each other's clothes by mistake. On their way back Sharmishta notices the error and asks Devyani why she has stolen her clothes. Devyani says it must have been in error. Sharmishta continues to accuse her of theft, saying her father was like a beggar who bowed to her father, the king, and depended on his charity to survive, and so on. It could've been a minor argument, as often happens among children, but Sharmishta takes it to such a degree that she ends up pushing Devyani into a dry well and she goes away in a huff. Devyani calls out for help and is saved by King Yayati, who happens to be passing by. Devyani thanks him profusely. By the time she is able to return, it is quite late, and she tearfully tells her father, Rishi Shukracharya, the entire story. The rishi says that since the king touched her while helping her out of the well, he is like her husband. This is episode one.

The rishi goes to King Vrishparva and complains about his daughter's insulting behaviour and how she said the rishi's dakshina was merely the king's charity. The king asks for forgiveness and says, 'My daughter will serve your daughter from now on.' The hierarchical position between the two girls is thus reversed, where the princess becomes the Brahmin girl's maid. Some days later, Yayati comes to meet the rishi and Devyani tells her father that he was the man who'd saved her from the well. The rishi thanks Yayati and tells him that he is now Devyani's husband. Yayati is sort of trapped into marrying Devyani. So he takes her to his palace. Her 'maid' Sharmishta accompanies them. The king falls in love with Sharmishta and she with him, and unknown to Devyani they have a relationship. So the king is outwardly married to a Brahmin girl, but his secret wife, junior wife—some say mistress—is the maid of the first wife, who is actually a Kshatriya princess by birth. Their status by marriage is different, and a rivalry starts between their children.

So, whose son will become king?

Exactly, that's the question. When Devyani finds out about the relationship and Sharmishta's children from Yayati, she is furious. She goes to her father and tells him that the king has betrayed her. The rishi curses Yayati and takes away his youth. Yayati instantly becomes old. Shukracharya's thoughtless curse causes his daughter more grief, since her husband is now old. So he modifies the curse and says that if a son of Yayati's were to accept his old age, his youth would return. That is, he can exchange his old age with his son's youth.

Yayati goes home and calls his sons. He asks Devyani's older son Yadu to exchange his old age with him. Yadu says it is adharma since the natural order is for the older generation to move on and the next generation to take its place. He does not accept Yayati's request. The angry king dismisses his son, ordering him to leave the kingdom; he curses him that his descendants will never become kings. Yayati's youngest son, Puru, is from Sharmishta. When asked, Puru accepts his father's request willingly. The child becomes old and Yayati gets his youth and virility back.

Sharmishta is upset and accuses Yayati of being selfish and greedy and uncaring of his son. The son accepted his father's old age out of his love for him. Did the father not care about his son's needless suffering?

Does Puru get his youth back?

Many years later, after Yayati is satiated with youthful pleasures. Some stories say that he finally realizes that there is no end to the desire for pleasure and becomes mature. He calls Puru and gives him his youth back. And although Puru is the youngest, he makes him the king. Yayati then retires to the forest. By that time, so many years have passed that Puru is already old. So Puru never experiences youth.

This is an ironical story where Yadu, the son who knows and talks about dharma, does not become the king. The youngest, who is an obedient son, but who is willing to change the rules of space and time, and dharma, becomes the king.

Is this Yadu the same one from the Yadava Vansh?

Yes. This is the seed of the story of the Mahabharata. From Puru arises the Kuru Vansh from which come the Kauravas and the Pandavas. Krishna is Yadu's descendant, so he can never become king because his forefather was cursed by Yayati. This is how the Yadava Vansh is always insulted.

Why is this story important? The Ramayana has an obedient son, and Puru too is an obedient son. What's the difference? Rama is obedient and dutiful for Ayodhya, for the kingdom. He is following the rules so that people know he keeps his word as is the custom of Raghukul. He does not do so for his father's pleasure, like Puru. What Puru does is not dharma because merely obeying your father is not dharma. It's all being done so that the king can enjoy the pleasures of youth. No one is even thinking about the kingdom. Only Yadu is saying this, and his descendant is Krishna.

Yayati was an exploitative father then?

In psychology, it's known as the Yayati complex. Sigmund Freud wrote about the Oedipus complex. Oedipus is a character in Greek mythology, who unwittingly kills his father and then marries his mother. The young defeats the old and establishes his authority; here, the young is more powerful than the old. The Yayati complex is the opposite, where the old exploits the young. It is said that this is the difference between the East and the West. In the West, youth is more powerful; in the East, it's the opposite.

Did Yayati also have a daughter?

Yayati's daughter is Madhvi, and this story too is exploitative and depressing. When she is born, astrologers predict that she will have four sons who will all become great kings. Yayati worries that these boys will end up warring with each other and it will create a messy situation for his kingdom. Once a rishi comes to him and says that his guru wants 5000 horses. Yayati says he has only 1000 horses, and offers his daughter. He tells the rishi to marry her off to any king who wants a son and buy 1000 horses from each as her bride price. The kings will each get a good son, and since the children will not be in one house, there will be no war. Basically, Yayati sells off his daughter. She is never asked what she wants.

After she gives birth to her fourth son, she takes sanyas. She becomes a great tapasvi. The four sons grow up to be great kings and come to the forest looking for their mother. When they hear her story, they want to go to war with Yayati. She asks them to forgive him. Meanwhile, Yayati has gone to Swarga-loka and all his punya, or good karma, gets used up.

He has to come back to earth, and wonders how to return to Swarga-loka. The gods tell him to seek forgiveness from his daughter. Madhvi says she's already forgiven him, and asks her sons to share some of their punya with their grandfather to send him back to Swarga. When her sons ask her how she can be so forgiving after everything her father did to her, she says it's all in the past. 'What would be the point of my doing tap if I couldn't forgive him.' So, while the king wronged his daughter, she sent him back to Swarga.

This story is not often read or told, and perhaps this is why the Mahabharata too is not read so much because of all these painful stories that are there in the epic.

YOU MAY ALSO LIKE

YOU MAY ALSO LIKE